# Searching for the Morning Star

# Searching for the Morning Star

Story and Illustrations
by
Shelli Jones

A Little Castle Book

Searching for the Morning Star
ISBN 0-89274-496-0
Copyright © 1988 by Shelli Jones
Sheldon's Limited Editions
c/o Harrison House Publishers
P. O. Box 35035
Tulsa, Oklahoma 74153

Published by Little Castle Books
A Division of Harrison House Publishers
P. O. Box 35035
Tulsa, Oklahoma 74153

Printed in the United States of America. All rights reserved under International Copyright Law. Contents and/or cover may not be reproduced in whole or in part in any form without the express written consent of the publisher.

## Dedication

To all the children young and old who dare to hold the dreams of heaven close at heart. May they find the courage to believe them and all discover the true glory of the Morning Star. I hope to see you in His Kingdom, brave explorers!

In His Love,

*Shelli Jones*

# Special Acknowledgements

## and Thanks

To Mr. and Mrs. James Forbes for their gracious grant, for availing their professional skills to me and for their many words of encouragement.

To those people who spent many tedious hours editing my first draft.

To my parents, Mr. and Mrs. David J. Jones, and my brothers and sister, Matthew, Mark and Meg. Thank you for the many childhood experiences from which I was able to draw and for the trips abroad and education which helped me in completing this project.

To all who in any way offered prayer and guidance – God bless!

# Contents

1. Shipwrecked ..................................... 9
2. A Most Amazing Place .................... 19
3. The First Trial ................................. 33
4. The Worry Wart .............................. 49
5. Prince Zip ........................................ 63
6. A Prophecy ...................................... 91
7. Trapped! ........................................ 119
8. Pilgrim Soup ................................. 131
9. The Power of the Sword ............... 157
10. Discovering the Pass ..................... 167
11. A Confession ................................. 179
12. Sweet Dreams ................................ 191
13. Battling the Sea Spirits ................. 211
14. Kidnapped! ................................... 223
15. Vanity Fair .................................... 231
16. An Adventure ............................... 247
17. At the Gates ................................. 269

# Searching for the Morning Star

# 1

# Shipwrecked

Clinging to the ship's mast, Castigio shut his eyes, shivering from head to toe! He was too frightened to move!

Lightnings flashed! Winds howled! Torrents of rain beat down upon the sea! Below the murky deep, ancient fountains bubbled and burst, surging upward to crest against the midnight sky. Towering waves swelled and broke over the dark waters of the ocean until its depths shook with their pounding. Sailing into its murderous clutches, the Spanish galleon struggled to stay afloat.

"Batten down the hatches! Pull in the sails!" yelled a crewman on the ship. Hatches slammed shut and sails fell flat against the deck. Everyone was scurrying to and fro except for Castigio who was hiding behind the masts and rigging. Storms scared him to death!

Sprays of salt water rushed over his head, knocking him flat upon his face! Sliding across the deck, he nearly slipped over the edge before grabbing a rail just in the nick of time!

"Great fish-flappin'-belly sprawlers!" he screamed. "We shall all be drowned alive!"

"Drowned alive! Drowned alive 'e says! Haw! Haw!" echoed the voices of the crew as they began to mock him. Their course brawls of laughter filled the air. Rugged and seafaring were they – pirates each and every one!

Quickly Castigio looked for a place to hide from them and from what he feared worse than the storm! He ducked under a fallen sail. Thunder crashed, then the rumbling of heavy feet running across the deck filled his ears. The footsteps stopped. He listened for a moment. Cautiously, he lifted a corner of the sail covering him and dared to peek out. A blinding bolt of lightning flashed overhead! For an instant a fallen sail hanging suspended above his head became transparent in the light. Through it Castigio saw the dark silhouette of the giant man he feared more than the storm approaching.

Castigio shuddered. "El Capitan!" he gasped. The hanging sail crashed to the deck as the ship tossed once more. Standing before him was the most wicked pirate who had ever sailed the seven seas!

El Capitan, large and stout, stood under the creaking mast and spars. He was dressed in not one, but in two blood red capes which flapped violently in the fierce wind. His tangled mass of black hair whipped like a nest of snakes about his face. Glittering through his hair, an Indian slave's silver ankle bracelet hung from his ear! With his jaw set, his mouth fixed in a grimace, and his eyes piercing straight into the eye of the storm, the pirate looked like a statue carved of stone. Then he moved.

Anchoring his spiked heels into the wooden deck, he sliced at the air with a sparkling jeweled saber as if he alone could frighten away the tempest. Indeed, El Capitan appeared more permanent than the ship's own mast. Castigio almost pitied the storm, for of the two – the storm and the pirate – he was sure the pirate was the more evil and could outlast. El Capitan was not a man to be crossed.

Lightnings flashed around the pirate, setting the half-lowered sails on fire! "Put it out!" yelled the pirate pointing up. Then with the tip of his saber, he snagged the belt buckle of a startled sailor and tossed him into the air! Flying past the flaming sail, the sailor reached out to grab it. Ripping it clean away, he plunged into the raging sea! Nervous laughter broke out among the crew as El Capitan searched for another victim. Castigio dared not move.

"Who shall be next? Ye spineless seadogs!" roared the pirate with a horrible laugh.

Every pirate jumped to attention to appear as fearless as El Capitan. Stepping back, the captain surveyed the prospects with a sneer. Quietly, Castigio peeked out from under the sail which still kept him hidden from view. In horror, he saw the pirate's boot step beside the very spot where he was hiding! Castigio held his breath as he felt the point of the pirate's saber scrape across the sailcloth over his back! All eyes followed the saber as El Capitan slashed the air with its razor-sharp edge.

"What are ye gawking at?" thundered El Capitan. "Get to work! Swab the deck! Wrap up the sails!" Crewmen jumped like whips to obey as El Capitan whirled about in every direction shouting out commands. Castigio waited for a chance to escape and when the pirate's back was turned, he fled for safer shelter.

"To the crow's nest!" El Capitan was screaming. Castigio glanced up at it as he ran by. High above the ship it wobbled in a gusty gail just as the vessel heaved to one side in the waves. Slipping and sliding on the wet deck, Castigio kept running.

Realizing that he had given out more orders than there were men to fill them, El Capitan stopped in his confusion. Then he snickered as one more name came to his fiendish mind, "Castigio!" he bellowed.

Unnoticed, the scrawny shadow of the man slipped away behind the pirate as Castigio scurried down to the lower decks as fast as his legs would take him! With not a moment to spare, Castigio had escaped the pirate's eye!

"Castigio! You scoundrel! Shake your bones fast and get to the crow's nest!" Castigio shuddered as he rounded the corner of the stairs. He leaped down five at a time to get to the bottom faster!

"Where 'er ye dreamer?" demanded El Capitan, throwing back the crumpled sail where Castigio had been only moments before. Fuming and fussing, the pirate tossed sails and rigging aside looking for Castigio. "Ye scallywag! No use to me at all! Shan't it be a good night this one, if at last we have lost ye at sea and rid ourselves of the burden of ye!" he threatened as he poked his saber into the frumpled piles of sails that littered the deck about him. "Blast my boots! Where 'er ye?"

When no answer came, the pirate became enraged. "Have we a deserter mates?" Grabbing a crewman by the neck, he sent him sprawling in the direction of the galley stairs, yelling, "Find him or ye'll share his fate as well when I get my hands on him!" Jumping to his feet, the man began the search calling, "Castigio! Castigio! Castigio!"

Soon all the pirates were looking for Castigio. Where was he? Down in the darkest part of the ship: its very belly, the bilge. Among crates and barrels stacked together on top of boards and ballast stones near a crossbeam under the bow of the ship, Castigio found a place to hide.

The mere thought of sitting in the crow's nest made him more seasick than ever. Each time the ship pitched and fell in the sea, his eyes rolled around in his head. As he dangled his legs from a barrel where he was sitting, bilge water swirled about his ankles. The stench was horrible. But the pickles inside the barrel had a worse odor of vinegar that made his head swim. Many times before, he had hidden from El Capitan in the pickle barrels when they were empty. Only now there were pickles in the barrels and the ship's beam had cracked, so that slowly but surely the sea was coming in to drown him!

Castigio wondered how much time he had left before either the sea or the pirates finished him off.

Lifting up the tiny stub of a candle he had grabbed from the stairs, he searched for the leak.

The crack was bad. Castigio decided to climb up higher on the barrels. But as he did, his foot slipped on a slimy patch of barnacles.

"Oh, doomed! Doomed!" he cried as he fell into a bilge water puddle.

Instantly, it was as if the sea had heard his remark, for suddenly it tossed the ship again, setting the stagnant water from the bottom to rolling. Splashing over the pickle barrels, it put his little candle out!

"Oh, no!" sobbed Castigio. "I didn't really mean what I said!"

But it was too late.

*Could it get any worse?* he thought. *Oh, dear me, it seems I've been saying that forever, and, curiously enough, it does get worse!* He sighed as he pulled his scrawny knees up under him and shivered a little. *Yes...Much worse!*

He sobbed as he sat there in the dark thinking of how he had come to be in such a miserable state. "Ah, my motherland, my queen, my dear, dear Spain. How I have failed you. I shall never be a great conquistador now – no never, not ever."

He recalled the day so many years ago when Spain had sent her young men away in search of treasure, spice and gold and the wonderful Fountain of Youth! What a wonderful vision it was, but alas his youth, how quickly it had passed away! That day seemed as though it had happened yesterday. Castigio remembered it as he would have remembered a holiday.

"Oh, doomed! Doomed!" he cried
as he fell into a bilge water puddle.

He could still see himself standing on the docks in a shining new suit of armor. Waving to the crowds, he had joined a great parade of brave explorers marching up the gang plank to their ship. Each had dreamed of returning one day in victory and wealth!

However, days at sea turned into years, and years into decades until at last the crew's dreams faded away and the ship was lost at sea. Castigio was quite certain that Spain had forgotten them all long ago.

Only Castigio continued to dream the old vision. But his armor did not fit so well anymore, because he had grown old and skinny. He had lost his courage too. But a dream truly believed, even in the heart of a coward, can lead a man into adventure.

One day El Capitan's ship had passed by them. There was extreme excitement among the crew. The pirate had introduced himself as a great explorer. Everyone of them believed all the tales of adventure that he told them except for Castigio who thought their happening upon him was just too good to be true.

The crew were too quick to turn their ship over to El Capitan and proclaim him their brave new leader. Castigio protested, but no one listened. Spellbound by the notion of pirating riches and conquering new lands, the conquistadors gave up their mission, dusted off their sails from years of drifting and readied themselves for high adventure. When Castigio reminded the crew of the glory of Spain and of their dream to find the precious Fountain of Youth, El Capitan mocked him for being a dreamer. Castigio became an outcast!

From that day El Capitan always found the worst sort of work for Castigio to do; he had him hung from a rope by his ankles over the side of the ship to scrape off barnacles and green slime! El Capitan enjoyed tormenting him and making his life miserable. Castigio's only escape was to hide!

But this time, escaping seemed just as bad as facing El Capitan and the storm. As Castigio sat and thought of all these things, an eternity seemed to pass.

"Perhaps I'll drown if this gets any worse!" the little Spaniard said to himself. He squinted his eyes to peer into the dark, but saw absolutely nothing! All he could do was wait and listen. He could hear the eerie creaking of the beam, as it continued to split, and the lapping of water against the barrels. Just then, he realized that all else was quiet except for that.

"Could it possibly be that we have survived this wretched storm?" he asked no one aloud and waited to see if it were so. Realizing that the storm must be over, he relaxed a little – but not too much. Castigio was still in quite a predicament. He could not see to climb out. Worse yet, the captain would surely be waiting to punish him!

Suddenly he heard a loud crack! The beam split wide open and all the ship above him shook.

"Oh, it's the end for sure!" cried Castigio.

"No, it isn't, you old fool!" yelled a voice from the dark.

Castigio shivered behind the barrels. So I am not alone, he thought.

"We have run aground on an island. We are going to march against its people and conquer them. Then we'll steal their treasures too!" said a greedy voice in the dark somewhere.

Castigio squinted and noticed that light instead of water was coming through the cracked bilge. The voice was right. The ship had stopped. He heard a shuffling of feet and ducked behind a barrel.

"Get up, you old coward!" It was the voice of the crewman who had been searching for him. He had a spear in his hand and pointed it in Castigio's face.

"Oh, mercy me! Mercy me! Mercy, sir!" Castigio whimpered.

"I ought to say I found you and win a favor for myself!" the crewman said, his chest swelling with pride. "But now El Capitan is busy preparing for battle, and you'll not interest him at all till it's done. Lucky for you, Castigio! Here! Take this, you ol' bag of bones!" he said, thrusting a spear at Castigio's hand. "Go fall in line, or I'll drown you right here! Get!"

Castigio grabbed the spear, slipped through the crack in the ship and scrambled to shore. He lined up with the others, soon lost in the crowd.

"Oh, thank you, somebody!" he said.

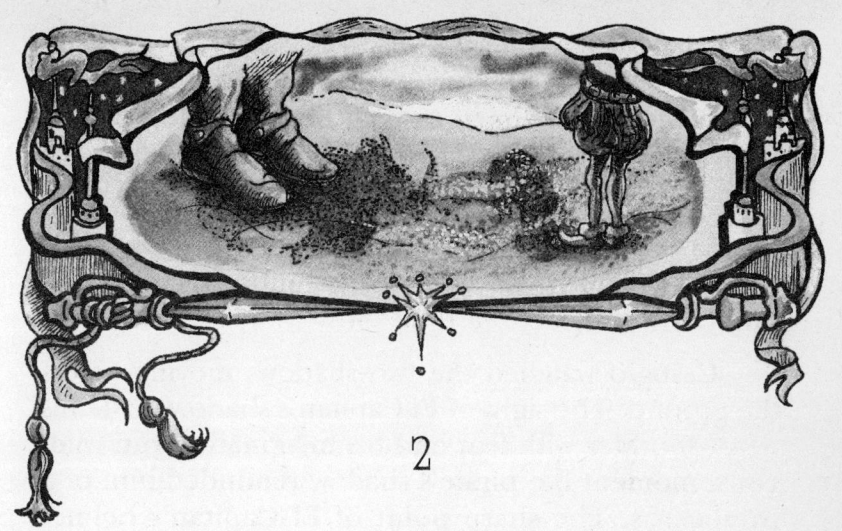

## 2

## A Most Amazing Place

Standing in line, Castigio wondered to what sort of place the storm had brought them. The sand on its shore was so loose and deep around his feet that he could not seem to stand up straight no matter how he might shift them to and fro.

He was busy trying to shake the sand and bits of seaweed off his socks when he heard the army bugle call behind him. The blast sent a chill up his spine, and his knees began to knock uncontrollably. He grabbed his spear and leaned hard against it, trying to appear not so nervous when the inspecting eye of the pirate passed by.

Soon the foreboding shadow of El Capitan did approach him. Castigio dared not look up above the brim of his tiny helmet. Instead he stared down at his feet and concentrated hard on trying to disappear or at least to seem inconspicuous.

"Teeny-weeny-itzy-bitzy-mini-me. Oh, my! Oh, why?" Castigio moaned as the gigantic shadow of El Capitan advanced toward his own.

Castigio watched the two shadows moving across the ground. The sight of El Capitan's shadow made his heart shudder with fear and his imagination run wild. For a moment the pirate's shadow reminded him of a rhinoceros. The sharp point of El Capitan's helmet became the horn of the rhinoceros and his bulging belly was the rest of the great beast. Castigio's own shadow seemed pitifully small in comparison. It resembled a skinny little walrus cowering helplessly before the charging beast.

Castigio nervously twisted sea water from his mustache and trembled for fear of his life as he watched the shadow of the rhinoceros run over the shadow of the walrus!

"Run for your life!" he screamed to his shadow. But he was too late. The shadow of the rhinoceros charged right through it!

"Oh! I can't bear to watch!" gasped Castigio shutting both eyes tight. He listened for the pirate's thunderous voice to bellow his name and waited to be seized for punishment of his escape.

Nothing happened! He waited. Castigio couldn't stand the suspense so he peeked open one eye expecting to see El Capitan glaring back at him. But El Capitan was gone – no where in sight. All that stood before Castigio was his loyal shadow, still in one piece!

Castigio looked around the line of crewmen marching with him. El Capitan was at the far end inspecting the last of his troops. The pirate had obviously passed him by, but why? Castigio wondered if perhaps he had been blinded by the sun and not seen him at all. He looked up at the sky, but found that the sun had yet barely risen. Castigio was astounded by his unusual luck.

For a moment Castigio stood there marveling at that. Again he heard the trumpet's battle cry, then the tramping of feet. Quickly he pulled himself together and followed in line.

It was then that he looked up to see where he was being led and realized that his eyesight seemed blurry. At first he thought the darkness of the ship's bilge, where he had spent the night, might have affected them. Then he supposed that the light of dawn settling over the island was bothering them. He rubbed them, squinted and blinked.

Again, he looked up and scanned the horizon to see where the army was marching. Everything seemed hazy, but Castigio strained to focus his eyes. "Blasted peepers! I must be going blind!" he said, propping open his eyelids with his fingers. Using this method Castigio could see miles of sandy shore and a range of mountains in the distance. Something moving slowly above suddenly caught his attention and dazzled him with its shimmering brilliance.

*Glory be! What is that?* he wondered. *Never have I seen anything so beautiful and magnificent as this!* He was not certain at first if it were some heavenly being or an unusual star. Its affect was most curious upon him, though, as he could not help losing himself in its mysterious glow. Its appearing seemed to ease the care of the battle and remove his fear of the pirate. In its presence Castigio felt a great flood of peace sweep over his soul as though he might melt. It was strange and yet even wonderful as if he had been befriended.

"Who are you?" whispered Castigio in fascination.

That same instant the brilliance flitted across a mountain ridge and stopped as if to answer him. It seemed to be beckoning him to follow its path.

"Wait! Don't go!" he called.

But it moved again behind the mountains, fading from view with the night. Pink rays of the morning sun rose in a misty haze in its place.

"What a wonderous thing!" Castigio breathed in delight. "I've got to tell someone! Everyone in the crew will want to know! This is better than pirate's loot! It's a real explorer's dream, a true conquistador's adventure to track that star! I wonder if anyone else saw it? If only someone will believe I did!" Castigio looked around for someone to tell.

But he was stunned to find that he was suddenly very much alone. The army of crewmen and pirates had marched off far beyond him while he had been stargazing.

"Oh! What mess have I gotten myself into this time? I am really going to have a hard time catching up to them now!" he fretted. "They will say I was daydreaming! This time El Capitan will hang me from the crow's nest upside down by my ankles for getting lost if he doesn't kill me first for running away! Mercy sakes! What to do? What to do?"

# A Most Amazing Place

Well, what was to be done about it? Castigio turned to run after them but tripped in the deep sand, falling face first. As his nose became buried in the sand he saw how it sparkled in the reflection of something bright. It was the amazing star!

"You are back!" he exclaimed. Castigio looked up to see the star again as it was slipping completely out of view. Day had broken over the island at last, and it was not so easy to see the star against the sky as at dawn.

"Wait! I must find you, Morning Star!" he shouted. But his moments of searching for the crew instead of the star had cost him time and distance. It was too late. The brilliance had disappeared from sight.

Castigio stood up and dusted himself off. He poured out the sand from each shoe as he thought of what to do. El Capitan was far away now and the battle was of no interest to Castigio anyway. Catching up with the others was out of the question, but Castigio did not want to be left alone either.

*I wonder if there are any sea monsters about this beach?* he thought and disliked being left alone all the more.

*Well, there's only one thing to do. I've got to keep moving!* He began to tremble in fear again.

*But where?*

Then a thought of thoughts came. *Why not in the direction of that star?*

"That's just what I'll do!" he said.

Castigio's feet were aching when at last he reached the foot of the mountains. As he did not know whether or not it was safe to sit and rest, he kept walking.

The closer he had come to the mountains, the more dry and barren the ground had become. And as he looked up to see how he might climb the mountain, he saw no sign of life anywhere. Far to his right was the sea. To his left was the direction of the battle. Straight ahead was a rocky summit that seemed to stretch all the way up to the sky. Castigio supposed that the star had led him away from the island's villages and people. The feeling of being lost began to haunt him and made his heart feel hollow inside. Again he searched over the awesome peaks of the mountains for a sign of the star. In its company he had felt a great deal of peace. If only he could see it again.

Night was falling once more, and Castigio knew that soon he could go no further without sleep. A gurgling sound in his belly reminded him that he was hungry too.

Just then he felt a shifting in the pebbles beneath his feet. Then a small explosion of dust swirled up to tickle his nose. He sneezed and sneezed and sneezed! In the commotion he heard a tiny squeak. Looking down he saw a ferret scolding him violently. He had been standing on the roof of its tunnel!

"Dear! Dear! What have we here?" Castigio choked on the dust. The ferret did not stay around for any conversation and scampered off in a flash to safety in the rocky slopes above Castigio's head. He watched it and for a fleeting moment thought of killing it for dinner with his spear. The only trouble was that he had never learned to use the spear properly and did not think he could kill the little creature anyway. Then the thought occurred to him that at least he might find a safe place to spend the night under a rock up there. So he chose a path and began to pick his way up the slopes to the top.

For hours Castigio climbed without finding any rock bigger than his toe under which he could spend the night. Finally, he reached the top of the first peak. He stood there catching his breath and rubbing his joints, still looking for a sign of the star.

The night was so quiet there. Up so high, Castigio thought he could hear for miles and miles if there had been indeed anything to hear. Straining his ears against the silence, he listened for even the faintest sound. He was not certain at first but then, he realized, "Yes! Yes! Yes!...I hear singing!" He listened more intently and definitely heard the sound of men's voices chanting as they do in battle. Castigio got so excited he did a little jig right up there on that mountain in spite of being so weary. As he did, he quite forgot his balance and suddenly lost his footing. Rocks began to shift and pebbles to clatter. Then a great piece of earth gave way altogether. Castigio toppled and rolled head over heels down the slope, banging his elbows and skinning his knees as he fell.

"Mercy me! Mercy sakes alive!" he cried. "Ouch! Ouch!-Ouch!-Ouch! Ouch!-Ouch!"

At last he came to rest, much worse for the wear of the quick journey. Castigio could not stop the ringing inside his helmet. The noise was making him half silly! Painfully lifting up a battered hand, he took the helmet off and let it drop to become a pillow for his bruised old head. It was there that he drifted off to sleep inside the cleft of a jagged glacier scar. As he slipped into sleep he thought that he could hear a distant army singing as it approached the mountains. "The crew...," he murmured supposing they had been victorious in battle and were returning to the ship. "...Must get back to the ship...," Castigio resolved, but was too exhausted to think about how to do it. "Sleep...," he whispered to himself.

How long had he been there? It was night. Was it the same evening or another after? Castigio awoke confused and cold. His stomach still reminded him that it was hungry and, oh, his head! How it bothered him! He reached up to rub it and found a large lump, the size of a goose egg.

Pulling himself up to use his spear as a crutch, Castigio saw that he was standing in a sheltered place inside the wall of what appeared to be a sort of canyon. As he looked down, a dizzy sight made him ill, for his fall had brought him to the very edge of a narrow cliff with not an inch to spare before he would have plunged over.

Down below was a churning bubbling river that showed no mercies in the path it took.

How was he ever to get down? Castigio studied his dilemma. At first it appeared that he was far from civilization and help. All he could see were rocks and ledges and more rocks. Then he began to notice that the rocks mysteriously turned pink on the other side of the canyon. As he strained to look, he thought that he could see them forming some sort of a wall. But the wall disappeared from his view behind a jagged rock.

*I've got to get to that spot over there if it's the last thing I do!* he thought, but then said aloud to himself,

"Don't say things like that!"

After some time, Castigio discovered there was indeed a way to reach the spot from which he desired to look. He backed himself up against the cold wet rock behind him. Then he inched his way around a curve on his tiptoes to avoid plunging off into the river. The rock was icy cold and slimy too, much like the inside of a cave! It was a brave feat for a coward like Castigio. But he was so frightened of falling that he didn't even realize how brave a feat it was!

At last he managed to grasp the rock ledge above him and pull himself up. Crawling across its flat top, he found a most amazing sight!

Bathed in a pale blue light was the other side of the canyon. And the mysterious pink rocks formed none other than the wall of a towering fortress. Its elaborate gate carved out of stone was laden with every imaginable jewel!

"Why, who could have carved such a magnificent thing way up here in this wretched place?" Castigio wondered aloud.

The detail was so overwhelming that Castigio could scarcely take it all in, for inside the walls of this fortress was an amazing city, built of every color of the rainbow. Even the sandy shores of the river were made of sapphires which sparkled with a blinding brightness. The source of the river was an enormous fountain that bubbled out upon a sea of glass.

A glorious array of banners made of silks and satins hung everywhere from the windows of the city's great mansions. It was as if a festival were being held. And the most inspiring sight of all was what delighted

Castigio the most! There, above the city and the fountain, was the Morning Star, shining with a light so bright that he wondered how it was he had ever been given the grace to gaze upon it. Within its beams of light danced tiny specks of color which absolutely fascinated him. It was almost as though the beams made music as well; but it was all so truly strange to him that he did not know for sure.

While he was looking at all the splendor, Castigio became aware of the sounds of an army once again.

*Oh, no!* he thought. *El Capitan has found me and will ruin this most wonderful treasure!*

As suddenly as he said this, a strange pang of guilt such as he had never felt before shot through his heart. He did not understand why, but he suddenly regretted what he had said about the pirate.

*I guess even a pirate would be stunned by the likes of this!* he thought. *Why, who knows, perhaps the heavenly beauty of this place could be the very thing to break his dark spell upon the crew!*

It was a sobering thought. Then he spied the band of men, much smaller than he had imagined by the sound of their voices. They were not his crew nor were they much like a real army at all. Instead they looked like peasants, filled with sorrow as they sang a sad funeral dirge not at all fitting for the splendor of that city. Castigio watched as the procession came winding down a far slope of the mountain toward the gate of the city. In their arms they carried a dead man, and as they stopped at the river before the gate, a beam of the star's bright light suddenly shot out to meet them, evaporating the waters of the raging river and opening a path for them to cross!

There, above the city and the fountain,
was the Morning Star.

Castigio choked, for it took his breath away. Still he watched, yearning to follow them inside. On they marched into the waters of the fountain. Curiously they waded about. Castigio puzzled over this. He had never seen such a queer little ceremony before. Then one of the men began to sing an anthem about the Bright Morning Star and to dance.

The star drew closer to them all as if it truly were pleased, and suddenly the dead man leaped off his stretcher and danced! Somehow he had been raised from the dead in the light of the star's wonderful glory! That was far too much excitement for Castigio. He fainted!

Hours later he awoke to see that a heavy fog had closed in upon the banks of the river and that daylight had replaced the magical moment of the night before. Great disappointment sank in his heart. He feared that perhaps the bump on his head had caused him only to dream it all.

"It's gone! How strange!" he said as he reached to feel the bump.

Castigio stared at the river below. Unfortunately, it was still there and he did not wish to cross it. Looking down the other side of the rock on which he had spent the night, he saw a more gentle slope that emptied into a valley many miles away. There, he thought he could see the faint outline of a village and the smoke of morning kitchen hearths circling up into the sky.

The thought of food tempted him greatly. He decided that for the moment he would rather be attending to breakfast than exploring. He would try to mark his path well and return to investigate later.

On the way to the village, Castigio had a little time to think, for with all that had happened his thoughts seemed not to be his own. He imagined himself to be the leader of men on a great expedition to find that miraculous kingdom if indeed he had not just dreamed it. And he imagined somehow having the courage to tell even El Capitan of all he had seen, because for the first time in many years the evil manner of the pirate did not haunt him as it always had.

"How crazy you must be, old fool!" Castigio said to himself again and again as he approached the village. But by the time he arrived, he had decided to carry out the strange thoughts in his head if ever the opportunity were presented. The image of the Bright Morning Star had consumed him.

3

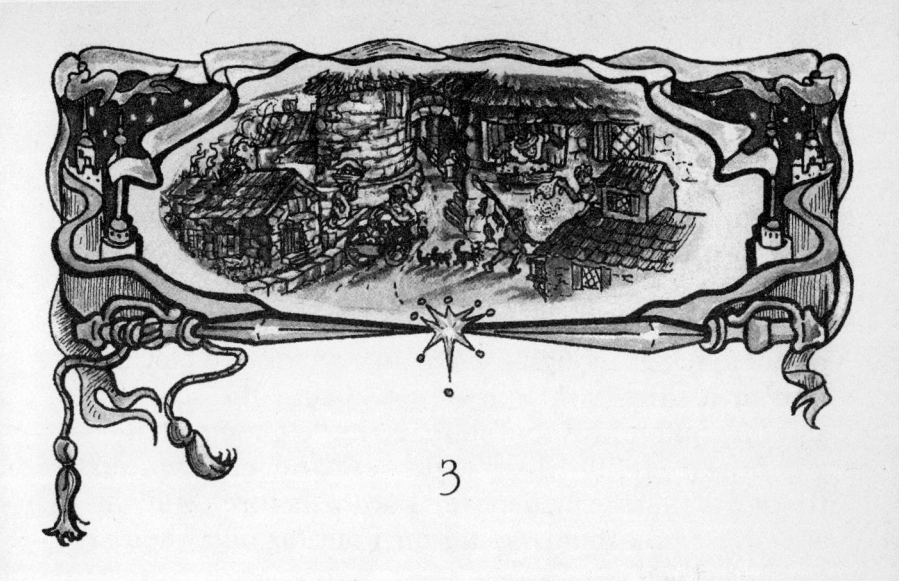

# The First Trial

The faint outline of a village that Castigio had seen in the early light of dawn was now becoming clear as each stride brought him closer.

*It will be filled with people,* he thought. At first the idea of company and food excited him and then again, *People...,* "he sighed with worry. He realized that the picture he imagined of himself as a leader and his adventure on the mountain might seem silly indeed to people in the village. The people might not be friendly either, and that began to frighten him a little. On that notion, Castigio stopped walking. Up on the mountain he had been so amazed at the sights he had seen that he quite forgot himself and his fears. But down in the valley the village began to seem large and he felt very small.

Little did he yet realize how changed a man he really was, for the Bright Morning Star was real and its transforming rays had touched him. He would never ever be the same again. It was because of the Star's effects that Castigio could not linger outside the village for long, as he would have chosen to do on his own. He felt as though some gentle wind were blowing him in its direction as it would against the sail of a ship. In spite of his foolish fears, he felt compelled to go on, strangely filled with new and courageous thoughts that he had never known before. Still, he wondered how things would turn out for him when at last he arrived.

It was no mistake that he should come to this place, for unseen forces were at work upon the village too. As blue evening darkness faded from the sky above the rooftops, so did the visions of slumbering men. Each dream and nightmare fleeted away on the wings of a magical breeze as it blew across the faces of peddlers and sailors to collect the last traces of the things they dreamt. Dreams of such things as fairy-tale castles with golden spires, knights and fair ladies with adventurous desires, and the cries of wild pirate battles mysteriously ended. The peasant's dreams disappeared from their bed chambers all at once. Quickly, the substance of those dreams sifted through thatched rooftops, rising high above the village.

Swirling together in a rainbow-colored mist of stardust, they rose up to the heaven beyond the mountains. There all the dreams paused a moment in the sky as if they did not really wish to depart so soon, but suddenly a great gust of wind swept them behind a moonbeam as it raced to the other side of the world where men were just then beginning to sleep. In the

# The First Trial

twinkling of an eye, the dreams disappeared just as if someone had called them all away. Their time was over and, sad as it was, it could not be helped for far below, the atmosphere was changing.

Streets began to fill with the sounds of creaking carts' wheels and peddlers whistling tunes. Windows flew open and shutters banged against the houses. Noisy happenings were going on inside, as plump peasant women banged iron pots about their kitchens in hopes of waking up their snoring, snorting husbands. Soon babies were screaming, cocks were crowing and bulls were bellowing; all in a miserable clatter. Nothing was pleasant. No one was smiling. Instead, everyone was frowning and complaining about what a wretched day it was likely to be.

These were the sights and sounds that greeted Castigio as he entered the little city. Walking down a cobblestone street, he traveled half in circles at times, first forward and then peering back over his shoulder as he tried to take in the scene. The confusion irritated him so much that he could not think. He crunched up his shoulders and tucked in his chin so that the brim of his helmet covered his ears and a great portion of his nose.

"Aa-aah," he sighed and relaxed a bit in the muffled quiet, all the while scanning the street under him for a stray piece of fruit that might happen his way from a passing cart. He had only a little coin tucked in his bloomers with which to buy a nibble. He was still very hungry. Soon exactly what he wished for came to pass. A nice shiny yellow pear rolled across his path. Quickly, he bent down to grab it. But, just as he did, a man's burly hands caught him by the seat of his pants and flung him through the air into a pile of baskets in front of a shop.

"Look where you're going!" yelled an angry peddler. Castigio looked up and saw that the man had plucked him away from the prized pear just in the nick of time as a team of horses came thundering by over the very spot where he had been standing a second before. Castigio watched in disbelief as their hoofs trampled his breakfast to pieces. He clamored up to retrieve it, but there it lay squashed – a yellow spot on the pavement!

"It could have been you!" mocked another passerby. "What were you doing doddling there? Dreaming?"

"Uh?...What?..." answered Castigio in a stunned murmur. "Oh, yes, yes," he said at last, "I guess I was."

"What?" said the crowd that had gathered to see what all the commotion was about.

"Uh...I was dreaming, I guess," said Castigio, still bewildered and hardly concentrating on the reply.

"Dreaming?" said the crowd in a whisper leaning closer.

"Uh...oh, maybe so, I don't know," agreed Castigio straightening his armor. All those faces staring at him were beginning to make him nervous.

"Dreaming!" shrieked the crowd. And as suddenly as they had surrounded him, he was alone, for they fled in every direction as if some monster had frightened them all away. Wide little ladies in kerchiefs and shawls covered their faces and ducked into doorways. Shopkeepers pulled in their carts and mothers bolted their shutters. Why, the town had suddenly shut up tighter than a turtle's shell. Castigio stood in the street scratching his bald head not knowing what he had said to cause such a ruckus.

"What an unfriendly lot!" he remarked to himself. "It's certain that I won't find breakfast here today! Where to go? What to do? Mercy sakes!" and off he wandered through the street not knowing what to expect next.

As he neared the edge of town, he again was thinking of the Morning Star, of his adventure, and of how he might one day tell El Capitan in boast, if ever they should meet again. These strange thoughts were beginning to amuse him as he knew that could never be. But still he resolved that if ever they should meet again, it would be the telling of the tale that would save his neck. He knew the pirate would be sure to punish him for desertion unless he could be distracted with news of some great treasure.

Castigio had begun rehearsing the telling of the tale when he came upon a tavern at the end of the street. It reminded him of breakfast again, and he wondered if it were locked up too.

*Well, there is only one way to find out,* he thought and tried the door.

To his surprise it moved easily on its huge iron hinges. As it did, the salty smell of bacon drifted out to assure him of the presence of the object of his quest.

Cautiously, Castigio crept inside. He was not yet certain that he would be welcome. Within a few steps he discovered that the tavern was dark, damp and musty. It was filled with drunk sailors whose awful singing echoed in each corner even at such an early hour. In the dim light, Castigio could not see their faces and this pleased him. He had not been noticed yet. He still had time to decide if he would like to stay.

There was a narrow aisle between all the tables and at its far end he spied an orange glow that he suspected might be coming from a cook's kitchen in the back. *This,* he thought, *would be the most likely place to find a scrap or two as I cannot afford to order a dish properly.*

Being small in size for a full grown man and bone-skinny, Castigio was accustomed to sneaking in and out of crowds when he wished, especially to avoid El Capitan and the others. So it seemed appropriate to him to avoid detection here as well. After all, why start more trouble? He had certainly had enough for one day!

Intending to crawl on his hands and knees beneath the level of the table tops, he started to bend over to reach the floor. It was dirty, and he slipped on a dripping of mush. Instantly a wave of laughter rolled throughout the place as he landed flat on his back, his clanking armor giving him away.

Castigio blushed beet red and slipped and crawled and kicked and slid as fast as he could back to the door. He had definitely decided not to stay! But the thick wooden door did not swing out as easily as it had swung in, and he found that he was unable to budge it at all. Turning around in a dither, he saw only one way out. He darted down the aisle toward the fire's glow, hoping to find a kitchen with a back door. Laughter followed him until he had turned a sharp corner and escaped into a narrow hallway.

# The First Trial

He could see the glow of a fire, but no one in the kitchen. There was yet an open door at the end of the hall between the fire and the tavern.

Castigio paused to fall against the wall and catch his breath. His heart was pounding fast, and great beads of perspiration were running down his face as he clutched his chest, shaking. He felt trapped between the humiliation of the jeering sailors behind him and the uncertainty of escape in the room beyond. But soon the laughter died away, and his heart beat a little slower.

He could hear the crackling and snapping of the fire in the next room. Warm blasts of air through the open door made Castigio begin to feel better. With curiosity urging him on, he peered around the corner.

There, standing before the fire was the familiar figure of none other than El Capitan! Castigio had happened in just as he was preparing to feast alone. What a fuss he was making! Bits of crusty bread crumbs flew through the air as he whisked them furiously away to clear the filthy table before him.

"Crumbs, spittle, stench and more crumbs!" muttered El Capitan, violently waving his hands across the table. A cloud of whole wheat dust encircled his head like a halo, causing him to cough in disgust. Then he crashed into his seat, shaking the whole table with his huge belly. A rat scurried out from under his feet, snatching up crumbs and squealing curses as it fled for dear life! Laughing wickedly, the pirate watched it disappear, then turned and froze with evil delight. Before him was Castigio cowering in the doorway!

"Well! What have we here?" El Capitan bellowed, his eyes flashing. "A crow from the crow's nest? Or a deserter from my ship?" he roared, leaping to his feet again. With one gigantic stride he stood towering over Castigio, glaring down at him. "Speak, ye Spaniard!"

Castigio opened his mouth to try, but it was of no use. He could not think!

"Come on now, ye rascal!" coaxed El Capitan, his lips slowly forming an evil grin that exposed all his golden teeth. Leaning a little closer he added, "I have stolen treasure to count – now ye wouldn't want to keep me all day..." (breathing in, he paused in silence for effect) "Aye...? Now would you?" he thundered.

His rumbling voice shook the answer right out of Castigio before he had time to think it.

"That's, that's just what I wanted to talk to you about," he stammered. "That's just the matter I...I...I...."

"What's the matter?" demanded the pirate.

"Fortune and treasure!"

"What about it?" breathed El Capitan in curious delight. The mention of treasure made his eyes begin to sparkle in an insane sort of way.

"I speak of something more important...." continued Castigio, realizing that indeed this subject might save his life for the moment at least. He would try hard to put more confidence in his voice.

"What is more important than treasure?" interrupted the pirate. "More than gold and spice?"

"A treasure that cannot rust or fade!"

"Where?"

"In the mountains...a fountain that restores dead men," continued Castigio. "One of the very stars out of the heavens! A blazing Star to guide our path in battle to victory and...."

"No!" thundered the pirate. "Ye idiot!"

Castigio stopped with a gulp. The expression on El Capitan's face had changed from greedy interest to trembling rage. The pirate thrust out his hand, grabbed the Spaniard by the throat and slung him down on the table with a slap. "Do not tell me that ye've come here to burn my ears with more of your ridiculous dreams! I hate them! Only fairy tales! I have heard enough about sea monsters, unicorns, and the Fountain of Youth! If that is all that ye have come to say, then babble no more!"

Castigio gulped again. Shrinking beneath the brim of his helmet, he thought frantically, *How can I make him believe me? This is different!* (The pirate's hands were tightening with impatience around Castigio's skinny neck.) Then from deep within his soul he heard a small voice, "Speak now!" it urged. "Speak now or die as a fool!"

So Castigio shut his eyes tight and blurted out, *"No! No! No!* It isn't like that this time! What I say is true!"

Still holding Castigio's neck, the pirate knit his black brows together. "It had better be!" he roared. Then he snickered into Castigio's face. "I would like some entertainment for my meal. So sing your tale for my amusement, or I'll stuff your mouth with apples like a pig and roast ye in this fire for my dessert!"

"Sing it?" Castigio choked, staring into the horrible buldging eyes.

"That's what I said ye scoundrel!" roared the pirate. "Now get to it!"

Castigio was so frightened that he could hear his heart beating. That scared him even more! But as he listened to it, he heard a beautiful rhythm pounding deep inside, something that he was certain he had never noticed before.

Indeed it was the melody of a song and it seemed to flood his entire being with a heavenly peace, just like the feeling he had had while standing in the presence of that marvelous Star the night before.

It was a wonderful melody much like the sound of a bubbling brook as it splashes and spills downstream along its merry way. The joy of it made Castigio forget his fear and want to sing. Before he knew what was happening, his tongue began to tingle as if hundreds of tiny sparks were lit inside his mouth and he could hear his own voice filled with verse as he began to chant his tale:

I had trudged through hidden alleys,
And climbed high above the hills.
I had marched through winding valleys,
Even slept through battle drills!

I had seen the isles of spices
And surveyed the courts of kings,
I had lost to men's devices,
Yet seen what victory brings.

"That's what I said, ye scoundrel!" roared the pirate.

Searching for the Morning Star

    I had found quite many riches
    And had strange adventures too,
    Even saw three ugly witches
    And once chased a baby kangaroo!

        But!

    Yesterday while I was list'ning
    To the army bugle's call,
    I saw far above it glist'ning
    A curious light, yet small!

    In spite of travels and career,
    Its kind was not discovered,
    So cautiously I ventured near
    To find out where it hovered.

    Above a rocky mountain scar,
    Shone its white and spotless face,
    A beaming, brilliant, Morning Star,
    Whose enchantment filled the place!

    Beneath its silent magic glow,
    Slept a city in her fort;
    Its jeweled gates barring any foe
    Entrance to the sacred court.

    Her streets, with golden ore were made,
    Near banks of a crystal sea,
    Where sand as blue as heaven laid
    Below a fountain flowing free.

        Then!

# The First Trial

Close by her jasper walls, I spied
A small band of solemn men,
Whose wretched manner was not pride
But that of soldiers beaten.

Straight past the splendid gates they came.
Weeping sighs rang through the air.
Each one hob'ling, crippled or lame,
Returned from distant warfare.

Upon their breast was hugged a corpse.
With gentle hands they held him.
But, in the fountain's bub'ling source
Danced queerly 'round about him!

On through that shining Star's bright rays,
Processed the mystery band.
Then to my blinking eyes amaze,
Leaped the dead man, 'oer the sand!

Splashing through waters, pure as dew,
He laughed in the merry light,
Followed by others, all made new,
Skipped, singing into the night!

We have drunk from living waters clear,
Mortal wounds, we keep no more!
Oh, Morning Star, whose beams are dear,
You have changed the battle score!

        Why!

In vain, I'd lived my whole life long,
To search for youthful pleasure,

45

And never chanted such a song,
Nor found a better treasure!

Castigio sat back, shaking with excitement. The secret was out at last! He was so overtaken by the telling of it, his toes were tapping a happy jig.

Reaching under the table, he found both knees bouncing. Grasping them tightly, he managed to stop the unruly feet at the other end of them. His skin was gooseflesh all over – only it was not from fear, but from pure joy!

Peering out from under his helmet, he eyed El Capitan anxiously. To his surprise the pirate was staring back with an empty expression on his face as if he too were miles away in that wonderful place.

"No stranger tale have I ever heard," he muttered to himself. Then he realized that the Spaniard had finished singing. Not wishing to appear weak or foolish, he promptly became his gruff old self again and sputtered, "Fountains of Youth and magic stars! How absurd! Even if I did believe in such hibbily-nippendosh, I would never waste my time searching for it. No! Not me!

"For gold buys wealth and spice brings pleasure!" He fumbled about for his capes. "Look for those other fantasies if ye will, but do not bother me again!" He made haste toward the door.

The singing of the tale had brought upon the pirate a strange effect that Castigio had never seen in him before. The Spaniard marveled at him in disbelief as El Capitan yelled back, "Stay out of my sight and away from my ship too! I have no more use for the likes of you!" and he left, forgetting even to punish him.

    Castigio watched El Capitan storm out of the tavern, throwing every sailor in his path into the laps of the others. A horrible fight followed. Broken chairs were hurled through the air above Castigio's head. He ducked in time as sailors followed after. Tables were turned over and mugs rolled to the floor spilling their brew. The entire tavern was soon in wild disarray. But Castigio sat still in the darkness. When at last they had all knocked each other out, he softly slipped away.

4

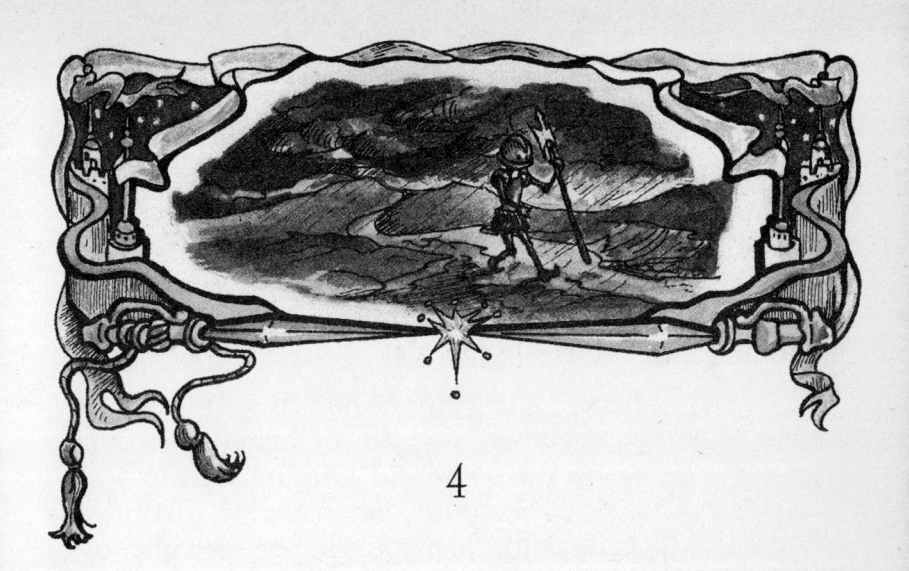

# The Worry Wart

The sky over the tavern was dismal and gray. Castigio watched heavy thunderheads roll across and smelled the scent of coming rain as he turned down an alley, then a street, and onto a dirt road. It was all very dark and gloomy, just the way he felt, by the time he left the city.

"Hibbily-nippen-dosh? Hibbily-nippen-dosh?" Castigio was saying it over and over again to himself as he shuffled along the road. "Whatever does that mean?" he asked nobody in particular and heaved a miserable sigh. El Capitan had indeed released him, but he had not believed the tale.

Rain began to fall in a steady drizzle.

"Pit-tip! Pit-tip!" was the irritating sound it made, hitting the top of his armor. Bothersome drops landed on his shoulders and slid across his back, spilling over the brim of his collar and all the way down his legs to the very end of his stocking heels. Then those sopping wet stockings bunched themselves up inside his shoes, rubbing with a horrible squeak.

Kicking first one heel then the other, he tried to straighten his stockings. In spite of his efforts, they stayed stubbornly the same. So limping a little and walking somewhat crookedly, he struggled to find a position where he could manage. He was very uncomfortable.

Shivering and cold, he ducked into his helmet. It was much too big for his wrinkled old head and slid down easily over his nose. Its dark dry space often afforded the only shelter that Castigio could find from the rest of the world. There he would spend hours and hours thinking about things just the way turtles do inside their shells.

*Did I see that Star or didn't I?* he thought, as the helmet clanked against his armor, spilling a puddle which dribbled down his mustache.

"Perhaps I really am an old fool," he said listening to the echo inside the helmet.

"Or perhaps I am not!" was the hollow reply. (The blasted trouble with helmets is that the echoes always get mixed up by the time they travel around inside your ears! This can be very confusing to those given to thinking aloud in them as was Castigio. However, having no one else to listen to him, he was accustomed to the sound of the faithful echo.)

## The Worry Wart

"What an old fool am I," he sighed, and the reply:

"Old fool, what am I?"

"Who knows?"

"Knows who?"

"Me, the conquistador!"

"Conquistador? No more!" teased the annoying echo.

" 'Tis true, 'tis true; El Capitan said it too," mumbled Castigio sadly.

"What is true, true, true...?" Castigio paused in the silence.

"I saw a strange Star!" Castigio said at last.

"And the Star saw you!"

"No! It could not see!"

"What could you see?" asked the echo impishly.

"A Fountain of Youth that made a dead man new."

"New? What made the fountain? Man?"

"Oh! I do not know!" confessed Castigio, growing a little tired of the conversation, but still the echo carried on, "What do I know?"

That was a puzzling question, so Castigio decided to think it over quietly for a while.

Of course, all this time, Castigio had been walking farther down the road and the rain had been coming down harder and faster. Now it was pouring in torrents. Castigio could not even see where he was going.

51

Not knowing where he was to stop, he decided to just trust his feet.

"Raining cats and dogs!" he said to his feet watching as they splashed through some deep ruts in the road. His feet were following a muddy stream that was trickling over them.

"Yep, raining cats and dogs," he repeated mindlessly, as people often do when they talk of such weather.

The words seemed to roll very nicely off his tongue, so he started singing them over and over in a senseless sort of jingle to keep himself company as he studied his feet and thought earnestly about the echo's bothersome questions.

"Raining cats and dogs! Raining cats and dogs..." and so he went along until all of a sudden something that smelled like mildewed wool who-o-o-shed right past his knees!

"Raining cats and...and...," he stopped, very startled.

Lifting up his helmet, Castigio peeked out to see what had sped by him. In the very next instant something pounced from the fog, sending him sprawling to the ground. Sitting up to his waist in a puddle, covered with dripping mud, Castigio stared down at a mysterious ball of sopping wet fur which had landed in his lap!

"Raining cats and...lambs?" blinked the bewildered Spaniard, leaning closer for a better look.

"E-eeck! It speaks!" shrieked a tiny voice from the depths of the tangled mass.

## The Worry Wart

Squirming and wriggling, it tried to dash away, but Castigio held it tight to make sure that it would not jump on him again once it was free.

"Oh, my hoofs and curls! My hoofs and curls!" it cried. "A barberry bush will eat me alive!"

"Barberry bush? I'm not a barberry bush!" said Castigio indignantly, for this made no sense to him. "Oh! Then have mercy on me, potato sack! Mercy on this poor lambkin!"

"I am not a potato sack, either," said the little Spaniard earnestly. "Well, then what right have you to look like one?" demanded the fuzzy ball as it began shaping up to be a lamb.

"I don't!" said Castigio confused.

"Yes, you do!" sobbed the lamb. "And I was going to hide inside of you until the rain stops!"

Castigio looked down at his dumpy bloomers and sagging socks. "Well, I suppose from your height up, it might appear to be so. But, I am not a potato sack, nor a barberry bush. It is all a case of mistaken identity!"

"A potato sack, maybe not; but a barberry bush...Yes, indeed!" contradicted the lamb.

"Not me!" said Castigio firmly as he stood up once more, shaking the lamb from his lap to the mud. "How ever could that be? Why I don't even know what one is!" he added thoughtfully, wringing out his mustache.

"Well, you are certainly just as rude!" exclaimed the lamb, shaking herself off and splattering mud all over Castigio's armor.

Squirming and wriggling, the lamb tried
to dash away, but Castigio held it tight.

"A barberry bush is a terrible thing and never have I known a worse one!" she explained. "They tempt you near with delicious red berries. Then when you are quite enjoying yourself they snag you in and clutch you tightly by their branches, so that there is no escape until the wolf comes. Barberries and wolves just go together in the most dreadful way. Nasty things! Nasty things!" she finished, trembling with fright.

"Um...now that you mention it, I did hold you rather fast, I must admit," Castigio said shyly.

"In the most genuine barberry style!" agreed the lamb.

"Oh, dear," sighed Castigio. He was feeling very trapped in the whole matter, just like a regular criminal. What was left to prove his innocence? He had never argued with a lamb before and was not sure which one of them was the wiser. *This is very tricky,* he thought as he ducked into his helmet to think the matter over a minute. "Oh, what ever shall I do?" he thought aloud.

"Oh, do whatever I shall!" came the ridiculous echo.

"Blasted helmet!" muttered Castigio, knocking it into the mud with his fist.

"Oh, my hoofs and curls! Wicked barberry bush! Naughty thing!" observed the lamb, dancing about in a fright.

"Do I look like a barberry bush?" asked Castigio in frustration.

"Well...no," confessed the lamb.

"Then that proves that I am not one!"

"Then what are you?"

"I am a man. That's what I am of course!"

"Nothing is proved at all," said the lamb, "Because you speak just like the bushes do!"

Castigio was getting more and more confused, and it seemed as if the situation was getting hopelessly worse. Then a bit of wisdom came to him in the nick of time, "Tell me now," he said, "when do these bushes speak to you?"

This question baffled the lamb. So it trotted in a circle until it could recall the answer.

"Yes, I know when," it said at last. "Just before I see the wolf hiding in them!"

"Ah, ha!" cried Castigio in delight. "Then it is not the barberry bushes that speak, but the sneaky, evil wolf, that lurks behind them. Don't you see how he just means to trick you?"

"Yikes!" squealed the lamb. "Then perhaps you are the wolf, and that is worse!"

"No, that is not what I am," said the Spaniard confidently, standing up straighter. "My name is Castigio – the man, the Spaniard, ex-conquistador – at your service, Lambkin!" With that he picked up his helmet and bowed graciously. "Now what is the name of the wolf?" he asked.

"It is too dreadful to say aloud. Draw closer so I can tell you softly."

Castigio obeyed.

"His name is Abaddon!" whispered the lamb.

"Abaddon!"

"Shhhh!" scolded the quivering lamb.

"What good news!" sighed the Spaniard relieved. "My name is not the same as his, nor his the same as mine. So that proves that I am not the wolf, and he is not the man!"

"Oh, splendid! How smart you were to figure that out indeed!" cried the lamb, leaping for joy. "Now there is no reason why we cannot be friends."

"But I'm afraid there is. You know my name and I have not heard yours."

"Oh, dear me, that's true," giggled the lamb. "Very foolish of me. I am called Soot by most."

"Soot? How strangely does that fit you, small friend, because soot is black like ashes. You are as white as snow!...Well...almost," said Castigio looking at the little white lamb splattered with mud.

By that time the rain had slowed down to a mere drizzle, and they could see each other much more clearly.

"I will tell you how Soot came to be my name if you want to listen, but it is a sad, sad tale!" sighed the lamb.

"I don't mind, if you can bear to tell it," Castigio assured her.

"Let us have a seat, then, and I shall begin."

They both plopped down in the road to have a good sit. Having fallen in a puddle before, they were not the least bit worried about soiling themselves.

"One day, a fortnight ago, my dear mother led me to the low pasture with all the other spring lambs to play. She warned me to stay with the others in the low fields, then went off to gossip with the other ewes. "Don't go near the hills or you will not hear the Shepherd call us home when it grows late," she warned me. And, oh, how I wish I'd listened, Castigio!" The lamb began to cry.

"There, there now, I'm listening, friend. Do go on," Castigio said, not quite knowing what to say, but trying to sound sincere.

"Well...," sobbed the lamb. "The older twins in our group thought it would be great fun to explore a shepherd's chimney in the hills up above. They said it was fun to roll in the ashes and let them tickle your nose. We all forgot our mothers and had a great time chasing each other up there. When we saw the chimney, we raced to see who would reach it first. I am a fast runner, and I won. I thought that I would make the others jealous by being the first to romp in the chimney ashes, so I dived in head first and stirred up a big cloud of ashes," the lamb stopped and was soon crying so hard that she could not go on.

"Then what happened?" Castigio coaxed. "Go on."

"The most awful thing," said the lamb. "I heard them all running, and I waited for others to jump in with me. But they never did. When the cloud of ashes died down, I saw them running the other way! 'Wait!' I cried, and started after them. One of the twins tripped me and pointed to my fur. "It's black! Black like soot! Soot! That's what you are? Soot! Ba-a-ah! Black sheep, stay away!"

## The Worry Wart

He began to chant, "Black sheep, stay away!" Some of the older ones joined in too. Just then we all heard the Shepherd calling us home. Everyone began to run down the slopes to answer him. Some of my friends came to help me, but that twin kicked them away and yelled, "Are you crazy? If the Shepherd sees her, he'll know where we've been and that we disobeyed. Stay away, black sheep!" and they left me. Then I was afraid to go home. I was ashamed of myself. I didn't want our kind Shepherd to be angry with me."

"And how did you meet the wolf?" interrupted Castigio.

"Well, after they were all gone, I went back to the chimney, buried myself in the ashes, and spent the night alone. I've been alone ever since. I was so scared! The next day I tried to find something to eat up there, but nothing grows so high up except barberries. I found some delicious ones and was filling my tummy when I caught my fur in a branch. I bleated for the Shepherd to rescue me, but I knew he could not hear me. Even so, I called. Suddenly a voice answered me, but it wasn't the Shepherd's voice. I knew right away, because it sounded evil. So I tore my hip in the bush and got away. I've been running ever since from a terrible wolf. And I ran all the way down this road until just now when I bumped into you!"

"How truly sad," sighed Castigio as he too wiped a tear from his eye.

"I miss my mother!" cried the lamb, "And I'm hungry!"

"I'm hungry too!" said Castigio.

"And I wonder if the Shepherd is looking for me? I'll bet his heart is broken, and it's all my fault. I'll never forgive myself. Never!" and she began to cry harder and harder.

"Oh, please, Lambkin, don't do that," the Spaniard pleaded, "You'll get me homesick too, and we'll neither one be any better for it."

The lamb was not persuaded.

"Why, look here, Soot! You see? While we've been here all this time talking, the rain has washed you clean again!"

The lamb looked herself over in disbelief.

"Now you could go home to the Shepherd if you knew the way, and he'd be pleased to have you again!"

"But I don't know the way. I'm lost!" The lamb had stopped crying.

"Well, then, I'll help you find the way," offered Castigio gently, for he was truly touched.

"Oh, you are too kind," replied the lamb, but she was delighted.

"No, I'm not," said Castigio. "I'm just lost myself, and I have nothing better to do. I was on a little adventure of my own, but no one believes in it anyway, so it is not really that important, I guess."

"You are marvelous to be so brave!" exclaimed the lamb.

"Me?" exclaimed Castigio. No one had ever called him brave before!

# The Worry Wart

"Yes! You're wonderful to help find the Shepherd and to protect me from the wolf!"

Castigio had not thought of that, but he decided not to let her know that a wolf might scare him too.

"Please tell me about your adventure since I have told you mine," said the lamb admiringly. "I will believe every word! I promise!"

Castigio was flattered. Her confidence in him had a strange new effect on his soul. He actually felt just a little brave and this puzzled him.

"I tell you what, Soot. Let us find something to eat before we are starved and vanish away, and I will tell you everything."

"What shall we eat?" asked the lamb.

"Well, berries sounded nice when you spoke of them. Perhaps we will see some on this road by and by!"

"Oh, I'd rather not," worried the lamb, "The wolf is sure to find me there."

"Don't be such a worry wart, Soot! You're with me now. We're together! See, I have a spear!" and he showed the weapon off in a true conquistador style as they started down the road again, though he'd never known how to use it.

61

5

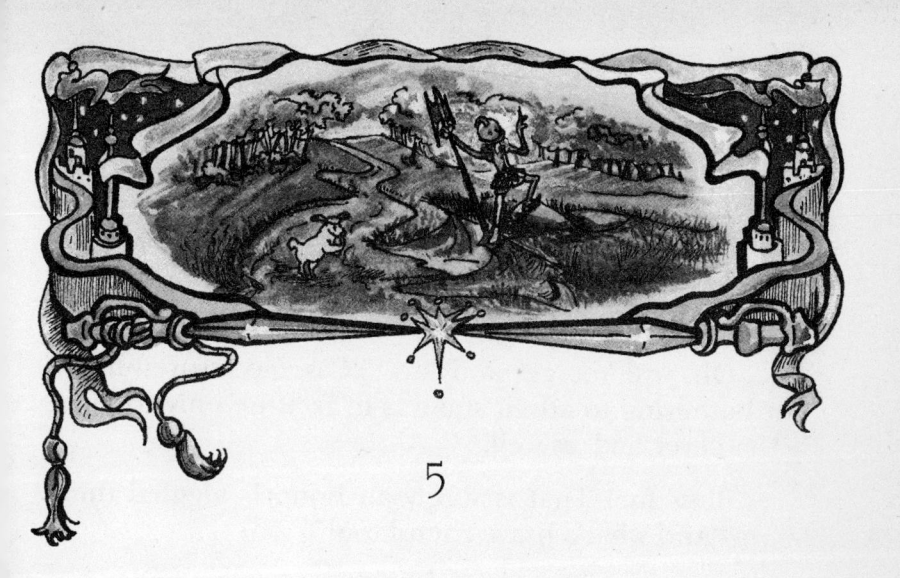

## Prince Zip

To any onlooker they would have been an unusual sight. The two of them strolling through the mud, a jingling suit of armor propelled by a spidery whit of a man leaning halfway over to one side as he conversed with a giddy little lamb who trotted in circles around him all the way down the road.

Soot was completely fascinated by the marvelous tale of the Bright Morning Star and its magical kingdom. Castigio was delighted when she begged him to repeat every detail twice or more. No one had ever paid any attention to him before this. As the afternoon came, and the road stretched on and on, they found they got along famously.

"Why, Soot! I must admit that you are the best friend I have ever had!" Castigio exclaimed as he finished his tale for the third time.

"Am I truly?" blinked the lamb batting her lashes and blushing.

"Oh, yes! You certainly are!" Castigio assured her, not bothering to admit she was in fact the only friend he had ever had, as well.

"Bless me! That is surely an honor!" giggled the lamb. "And what a brave friend too!"

This flattered Castigio greatly and prompted him to make a little speech, for he did not see why he should waste such an opportunity on modesty as the chance might never present itself again.

"I pledge my heart's full devotion to you, my friend! We will be comrades to the end!"

"End of what, Castigio?"

He had not thought of what. The words just seemed to fit the occasion and sound like the sort of thing he had heard people say at some time or the other.

"End of...of...."

"End of the road?" squeaked the lamb. "Are we only friends till then?"

"Oh, no! No! No, Lambkin. Friends to the end. It's just a thing people say. Uh...It means to the end of life!"

"Ooh! How sad," sobbed the lamb as a big tear appeared and rolled down her pink nose.

"No! No! No! I didn't mean to make you cry, Soot! I'm not thinking about such things. Why, we're going to be friends for a long, long time!"

"Are you sure?" she asked.

"Well, yes! Till the end! Um, no! That's not what I meant again!"

"Then what do you mean?" puzzled the little lamb. "Are you my friend or not? You have such trouble making up your mind!"

Castigio would have agreed, for talking to a lamb was no easy thing. "No! I mean we shall be friends to the end of the journey! To the fartherest side of the earth, to the greatest length of the sea, to the other end of the rainbow!..." Castigio was getting carried away, and the lamb swooned with admiration as she studied his noble pose. Running up the bank of the road, he climbed upon a rock and lifted up his spear to the sky, "We shall be friends to the height of the stars, to the breadth of the wind! No foe shall part us, no enemy win!"

"We are like an egg and a yoke! A tooth and a grin!"

"A smile and a dimple!" added Soot quickly, not wishing to hear the valiant pledge come to an end. That was all the inspiration Castigio needed to continue.

"We are like birds in a nest!"

"Fish in a net!"

"Bees in a hive!"

"Honey and a dribble!" added the lamb dancing on her tiptoes.

"Chocolate and a nibble!" shouted the Spaniard!

"Butter and bread!"

"A needle and thread!"

"Berries and jam!"

"Oh, how hungry I am!" sighed Castigio.

"Oh, me too. Why did you have to say that?"

"I don't know. It seemed to come next after berries and jam. We were looking for berries today were we not? It seems like ages since I last ate," and his stomach agreed with a growl. "You see?"

Soot nodded her head sympathetically. "Well, then, we shall starve together if we must. It is at least comforting to know that we are friends, just you and I."

"At least that!" agreed Castigio. The reminder of food had dampened his spirit. "I suppose we shall find something by and by but just now I can't go on, Soot. We have been hiking forever, it seems. I can't go on a step farther." Not bothering to look beneath him he plopped down on the side of the road to stretch his legs.

"Mercy sakes alive! Scratch-patch-it!!!"

"Yikes!" squealed the lamb running to his side, "What is it?"

"Briers and brambles!"

"Yes, indeed! Prickly stickly ones!" Soot observed, as she helped him to his feet. His yellow stockings and the seat of his bloomers were covered with green thistles. Castigio felt just like a cactus. He looked like one as best he could tell, as he stood there staring down at himself in pain and disbelief.

"Where did this brier patch come from?" he yelled.

"I guess we were so busy talking we didn't notice," said Soot calmly. "But look up there, Castigio!" She pointed with her nose to a thorny cluster that ran for quite a distance along the bank above them. "My hoofs and curls! My hoofs and curls! It's a barberry patch, friend!"

"And I have half of it on my back!" remarked Castigio ignoring the importance of such a find. He had already begun to busy himself plucking out the thorny bristles one by one.

"Castigio! Castigio! Don't you see?"

"No, I don't," mumbled the Spaniard. "Just help me get these stickers off!"

"The thistles belong to berries! We can eat berries! Big red juicy ones!"

Her words eased his pain as Castigio was more hungry than anything else.

"Hurry then, Soot! Help me get out of this mess, so we can climb up there! Hurry! Yes! Let's do."

Soot's round cloven hooves were not very nimble at peeling off stickers. Instead, she bit at the stickers and tugged hard at his bloomers for they were pinned tight against his underwear. This did little good, but not knowing what else to do, she persisted until suddenly she ripped the whole bottom away in one jagged tear!

"Yikes!" she squealed through her teeth. Castigio turned to see her behind him holding the entire seat of his bloomers in her tiny mouth. But when he saw it, he could not help laughing at himself at last.

"Oh, Soot! I suppose that I am quite a funny sight by now! What do you say that we forget this task and be off to gather those berries! Trying to pull out the stickers could take all day!" With that they ripped off the rest of his bloomers and threw away the stockings too, laughing to themselves as children often do after muddying their clothes at play!

By the time he and Soot left the clothes behind to scramble up the bank for the berries, Castigio, clad only in his underdrawers and armor, had made a ridiculous spectacle of himself. It was a good thing that the afternoon sun was shining hot upon them, for Castigio's knobby knees were bare. But his appearance mattered little to either of them as they gorged on the berries.

Juice dribbled down from Soot's mouth over her belly as she happily stuffed herself full of berries. She had completely forgotten about how wolves and berries go together.

"What a scrumptious delicacy!" she said to Castigio. He cautiously pushed his way around a thorny bush behind her, for he had already picked one clean.

"A true delight! I agree! Ulp!" Castigio was about to comment further when his ear caught the familiar sound of bees.

Suddenly the lamb ripped the whole
bottom away in one jagged tear.

"Hummm! Hum-hum! Hum-hum-HUMMM!"
"Oh, my, did you hear that, Soot?"

"No! I wasn't listening to anything. I was just concentrating on these beautiful berries! Shhh! Let me be, Castigio. I see quite a lot to eat over here," she said, ignoring him as she carefully stepped over a thorny branch to take another nibble.

"Well, I did! I heard bees, and I'll just guess that they are on my side of this patch as luck would have it!"

"What kind of bees?" asked Soot, not truly caring. "Most bees won't hurt you if you are quite polite and leave a few berries for them too."

"Well, they're just bees, I guess. Any ol' bees. Just don't like bees buzzing around my knees," replied Castigio as he peered around the bushes for the hive.

"Buzz, buzz, buzz-buzzy-buzz-buzz-a!" said a voice behind him. Castigio danced up and down nervously, trying hard to see where the insect might be lurking to sting him.

"Hum! Hum! Hum-a hum!" sang the voice in an unusual bee tune.

"Ouch!"

"Did it get you?" Soot was by his side in a flash.

"Oh, yes, it did!" Castigio nodded, rubbing his leg.

"Well, where is the rascal then?" asked Soot, now taking up the search herself.

"Blasted! Can't tell!" Castigio shrugged, looking around quickly to find the bee before it stung him again.

Prince Zip

Castigio heard a rustling. They both saw something big and yellow flash through the leaves. They stopped to listen, then looked at each other.

"That must be a big bee!" Soot said.

"Hum-a buzz-buzz!" teased the bee voice again.

"It's coming from the other side of the bank over there, I think," Soot said taking a cautious step. "But why don't *you* go see?" Castigio clutched his spear a little tighter, cleared his throat and said, "Well, I'd better just take a look, I guess," and paused..."Hadn't I?"

"Yes, of course! But do be careful, Castigio!" The little lamb bit her lip and held her breath as he disappeared over the bank. She strained to listen, hearing neither bees nor any other noise. Then, suddenly, she heard Castigio shriek. She waited, frozen in panic. Had he found a beehive in the worst possible way?

Soot heard the bee voice again.

"Buzzy buz bizzzz," and then, "Ha ha a-a-a-a ha! Ho ho!"

She jumped as Castigio yelled, "Oh, ooh! No-Ooo!" Then, "A-ha-ha-ha! Eh e-e-h! Oh! Hyo hyo!"

"Buz! Bizz-bizz-bizz!...Bee-bee!"

Soot was bewildered. "Castigio, are you in pain or have you taken leave of your senses? What goes on there?"

She heard only blasts of laughter. There were two voices instead of one. She forgot her fear and ran over the bank to take a look. There at the bottom was the Spaniard rolling on the ground, grasping his belly with both hands and laughing as hard as he could. "Cut it out there! O-oo! It tickles! Yes, it does!"

71

"What tickles?" demanded the lamb seeing nothing at all around the Spaniard.

"Me! Hee! Hee!" announced a loud voice behind her. She spun around in time to see a furry tail bounce away beneath the bushes.

Leaping to Castigio's side, she yelled, "Yikes, the wolf! Castigio run!" Then, as she whirled to dart off through a field, a shadow of something pouncing above her head crossed over her. Her escape was cut off when the creature landed at her feet. She nearly fainted before she realized the creature was no wolf at all.

"Buzza buzz!" mocked the voice which belonged to a fuzzy orange lion cub with huge button eyes and an impish grin. "Why, you're not a wolf or a bee!" exclaimed Soot in astonishment. "Not me!" shouted the wiry thing gleefully!

"Why, you're just a cat!"

"I am at that! A lion cat! To be exact!"

"Then why were you impersonating a bee?" scolded Castigio, coming to his senses. As he straightened up his armor and adjusted his helmet, he began to look the rude creature over suspiciously. "Aren't you a bit big to be a bee?"

"Of course!" admitted the cub with a mischievous twinkle. "And aren't you rather silly to be playing soldier in your polka-dotties?"

Castigio looked down at his underdrawers, now speckled with berry juice in a perfect polka-dot pattern. He crossed his knees tight and blushed.

"Oh, he can explain," offered Soot sharply, for she was growing rather irritated with this fellow.

"Of course, he can! Scratch-patchet! Scratch-patchet!" mocked the lion cub. Then he hopped about plucking at his tail, pretending to be full of stickers as Castigio had been along the road. Castigio and Soot stared at each other in amazement, "You mean you saw us there?" they gasped in embarrassment.

"Yes! Yes! Ha! Ha! Ha!" he laughed. "I did at that! I saw you coming and scattered the path with sticker branches upon which you sat! You did it all just right! It was a terribly funny sight!" With that remark the joker completely lost himself in his own folly and flopped upon the ground in shrieks of laughter.

"He has made a joke of us, friend," mused Soot, feeling hurt for her new found companion. "Are you just going to let him get away with it?" She was hoping to see some action because of the brave speech Castigio had made before.

"I suppose not," he said, feeling very much on the spot to defend their honor.

"What are you going to do Castigio?" Soot spoke softly even though she need not have bothered, because the cub was still enjoying the spoof to the fullest all by himself!

"I don't know...," Castigio fumbled about, unable to think of a thing. A situation like this had never happened to him before.

"I know," Soot whispered. "This calls for a duel!"

"A what?" gasped Castigio, hoping that she had not said what he thought he had heard.

"A duel!" exclaimed the lamb proudly.

Castigio could feel goose bumps begin to spread over his skin. He wondered how he was ever going to get out of this. Then a saving thought struck!

"It doesn't have a weapon, Soot! You can't attack a beast without a weapon, if the duel's to be halfway decent and fair!"

Soot was disappointed for a moment. Then she figured out a way to save her adventure and their honor. "Look, Castigio, the nasty thing has already had first swing at us in the bushes. It's only fair to take our turn next. It has dastardly talons for claws, which is weapon enough!" she described dramatically.

"It's only a kitten!" Castigio still had a chance to back out, but the lamb would not be dissuaded.

"Claws are claws. Besides, that beast deserves what's coming to it." Turning backwards, Soot, with a little kick, booted Castigio forward! Awkwardly, he recovered his balance and aimed his spear, not knowing what to do with it next.

"Dastardly foe, take cover!" shouted the lamb as she cheered Castigio on. She could afford to be brave from the bushes! Startled, the cub bounded to his feet unaware of anything meant against him.

"Hey! Hey! Hey! Put that thing down! I was just fooling!" he stuttered, backing into a barberry bush. "Owe-ee!"

Castigio would have gladly put down his spear if it had not been for his new admirer pushing him on. Around the cub he circled, hoping that it would surrender. He didn't want to kill it. Its silly grin began to fade and a look of panic filled its shiny green eyes as it stared back at him.

"Fizzle its fur!" yelled the lamb.

"Oh, mercy sakes! Soot! I can't do it!" sobbed the Spaniard as he tugged at his collar. His suit was becoming sweaty inside and his knees were shaking hard.

"Friends to the end!" called the lamb.

"To the end!" choked Castigio and closing his eyes lunged blindly toward the cub. In an instant they were falling upon each other, but not upon the dirt with a thud. Instead they just kept falling. They had tumbled into a hole hidden behind the bush where the cub had been stuck with thistles. Castigio's eyes shot open to catch a whizzing glimpse of roots and dirt clods caving in around them as they fell.

"Oof!" They hit bottom like two flour sacks. The wind was knocked right out of them both.

Soot could not believe her eyes. Castigio and the cub had disappeared in a twinkling. Scurrying from her hiding spot, she ran to the hole and stared down into the blackness.

"Well? Who won?"

"Neither!" came the muffled response.

"Whose voice are you?" she called back.

"Either!" they both said at once.

"Oh! Well, come on out will you? We need to settle this thing!" said the lamb impatiently.

Castigio pulled himself up on his elbows and felt around for his spear and helmet.

The cub felt himself for broken bones. "Haven't any!" he announced at last with a sigh of relief.

"Any what?" asked Castigio as he dusted himself off.

"Broken bones."

"Oh, me either," Castigio said after feeling to see.

"Lucky thing for us both!" said the cub standing to his feet.

"Yes, it certainly is," Castigio agreed, not remembering their tiff for the moment.

"Say there, man, you weren't really going to use that awful thing were you?"

Castigio felt truly guilty and hung his head in shame. He wished the spear were smaller so that he could at least tuck it away out of sight.

"Certainly he would have," interrupted the lamb as she eavesdropped from above.

"Oh, well, that's all right. To be expected, one might. Assassinations are all a part of the game for us royal folk, you're not to blame! I'm going to grow up to be King of The Beasts someday! A blue blood all the way! And you can bet I would have shed it bravely!"

"Ugh! Not me!" said Soot squeamishly for the thought of blood made her dizzy. It had not occurred to the silly lamb that duels should end that way.

Prince Zip

"Life is full of chances," quipped the cub. "You might as well take them as they come and fun away the most of some!"

"Well, that's fine for you to say! You're not missing your britches or scratching your itches from a pinch somebody imitating a bee gave you!" Castigio rubbed his leg again. "And look at this hole we fell into. You've gotten us into a fine mess. Just how do you expect to get out?"

The cub looked up. The way out was far above them. He began to feel halfway sorry for pulling his pranks. He began to pout.

Castigio was surprised to see the look of concern appear on the cub's face. He decided that he liked the ornery creature better as it had been before. "Aw, come on now. Cheer up there. There must be some way out."

"Well, I don't see how!" the cub replied.

"I do!" came the echoey shout from the top. Soot was growing tired of waiting up there all alone. "You can stick your spear into the wall halfway up Castigio. Then jump up and grab hold. You can chin up on it. The imposter can climb up your legs and over your shoulders to stand on your head. Then I shall reach down and help pull him out. You can catch hold of his feet and follow after."

"Splendid!" Castigio was proud of her. Turning to the cub he shouted, "Stand back!" Then he spread his feet apart for balance and aimed to thrust his spear high. The great plan would have worked without a hitch except that Castigio's feet began to slip out from under him. He pulled them straight together, shifted himself for balance and took aim. As soon as he raised the spear, his feet slid away again. Soot began to wonder what was taking so long.

"Did you hear what I said? Will my plan work?"

"Yes, it could," the Spaniard yelled back. "Except something is slippery down here!"

The lion cub grabbed the spear and spoke up. "Let me try!" Stepping into a spot of sunlight that shone directly through the opening above, he took aim to cast the spear into the muddy wall over their heads. Alas! He slipped on his tail and fell on his back.

"Burr!" shivered the cub. "No wonder we're a-slipp'n and slidd'n down here. This place is covered with ice, my dear!"

"Ice?" Castigio moved into the sunlight too and bent down to have a look as well. Sure enough, his own reflection shown like a mirror inside a frozen puddle.

"What are you talking about?" demanded the lamb. "It's scorching hot up here." Indeed it was, because the sun had been rising higher in the sky the whole time she had been waiting.

"I do believe we're in some kind of cave!" Castigio answered as the cub sniffed the walls and licked at them with his tongue. "Soot, hunt about up there. Will you, Lambkin? See if you can discover an entrance. Perhaps there is some other way out of here." Obediently she darted about, pawing at the bushes to look for a hidden opening.

Meanwhile, Castigio and the cub began to keep each other company as they were uncertain of the length of the wait.

"What shall I call you?" Castigio asked.

"Prince Zip Von Zippilen III is my rightful title!" said the lion cub as he fluffed up his golden mane and puffed out his little round chest with pride.

"Your title?" asked Castigio.

"Yep! I made it up to fit my destiny!"

"I see," said Castigio.

"I am an orphan! Are you?" quizzed the cub stretching his limbs and arching his back.

"No, I'm just lost," answered the Spaniard thoughtfully.

"Oh, I'm lost too."

"Well, how about that! Now we have something to talk about. Do go on, Your Majesty."

Prince Zip was pleased to have the audience. "I have been on my own as long as I can remember...."

"Here? In the brier patches?" Castigio interrupted.

"Oh, no! I only passed by here today, a short while ago I'd say. When I saw you coming, it seemed like time for funning, so I decided to stay! Hee hee! Ho! Ho! Hay! Hay!"

"Yes, yes, never mind that part. I know it already!" snapped Castigio not wishing to be reminded of the spoof again. The humiliation of sitting there on the ice, shivering in his polka-dotted underdrawers was enough of a reminder for him. "Get on to telling where you came from," he urged hastily.

"Uhmm! Yes, where was I?" asked the cub covering a silly grin with one paw.

"You were about to say where you came from and how you got to be an orphan."

"Oh, I don't know how, but I come from the forest now."

"What forest?"

"The one where the owls found me."

"Oh, I see," said Castigio again, but he didn't really understand whether or not his question had been answered at all. He was just being polite. "Do go on," he coaxed the cub who was beginning to get annoyed with the interruptions.

"As I was saying," he scowled, "The owls found me wrapped in a purple robe there in the forest."

"How did you get to the forest?" asked the Spaniard trying hard to follow the story.

"I was too young to remember," said the cub firmly, becoming more aggravated with the nuisance of another question. Castigio decided that he would try hard not to interrupt again, but the cub being offended began to pout. "Oh, dear! How rude of me. I beg your pardon." Castigio pleaded.

"No use! See what you've done? I've lost the rhythm and the rhyme. Telling it now would be a waste of time," scolded the cub.

"No, you didn't! Did you hear what you just said? It rhymed! It rhymed! Go right ahead!" exclaimed Castigio.

## Prince Zip

"You're rhyming too. I want to know how? This trick's not for you! Stop it now!" demanded the jealous cub.

"I...I...I'm sorry...I was only listening to you and now it seems quite easy to do," Castigio tried to apologize.

"You're confusing me! Rhyming is only for royalty!" said the angry cub stomping his foot to emphasize the point.

"Says who? You?" said the flustered Spaniard.

"You must stop now, I say! We can't go on this way!" wailed the cub with his hands over his ears. Castigio saw a tantrum coming on and decided it was cruel to have spoiled the little cub's fun. Slapping both hands over his mouth to resist the next temptation to speak, he marveled at how catchy the rhyming was.

"Rhyming is only for the royal few. It's the sophisticated thing to do," sobbed the cub. "Isn't it?" he asked, looking at Castigio who was beginning to feel sorry about the whole incident.

"Uh?...Oh, yes, yes. Of course it is," Castigio assured him. He realized that the cub must have made up the game when he was alone in the forest. "Go ahead and tell me the rest of your story."

Prince Zip eyed him suspiciously. "Are you sure?" he asked.

"Yes," said Castigio pulling his hands away from his lips only long enough for one word to slip out. Lest he speak another rhyme, he quickly slapped his hands back over his mouth again.

"Where was I?" The cub searched for a starting place.

"Owls," Castigio reminded him.

"Oh, yes. Ummmm. AH-hummm." The cub cleared his throat and began. "The owls just found me in the forest beneath an old oak tree. I was wrapped up in a purple robe as royal as could be!"

"Couldn't they find a clue about who made the robe or what village it was from?"

"No!" Prince Zip answered crossly. "A great white eagle flew into the woods that very night and snatched the robe up in her flight! She flew to the mountains with it in her beak, where her chick nestled it like a swaddling cloth against its cheek."

Castigio was so interested he could not seem to stop asking questions. But it was obvious that the would-be prince only wanted to tell the tale in his own way. Castigio settled back again and pulled hard on both ends of his mustache to remind himself of his vow not to interrupt.

The cub continued. "Purple is the color of royalty, you see. So the owls believe that I am of royal lineage. As royal as can be! That's me! Hee! Hee!"

"A real prince!" said Castigio in amazement.

"I know it's true because I met someone in the forest who told me my blood was blue!"

"Who?" asked Castigio without thinking. Then he remembered quickly to add, "Excuse me!"

So the cub went on, "In a dream I saw a maiden there. She glided about as if on thin air. She brought a flute up to her lips, but instead of playing it, sang a song that went like this:

> "Behold the Morning Star in yonder place,
> where eagles fly with wings of grace.
> Beyond the mountains is their nest
> wherein a city finds her rest;
> A magic city all of gold
> whose gates are guarded by lions bold!"

"A star?" Castigio's curiosity was beginning to bubble uncontrollably at the mention of the Star. It was all he could do to keep from making another outburst. The cub was glaring at him from the corner of his eye waiting to see if indeed he might go on, then he continued reciting the song:

> "Enemies the kingdom had
> like wolves and buzzards and men gone mad.
> Kidnapped from the royal guard,
> a destiny in life was marred.

"She was about to tell me more about my inheritance, I'm sure. But the owls awakened me from my rest and put me to work guarding their nest. I told them of her lovely song. They warned me that the road to the mountains was too long. I vowed to find the way, but they said I'd have to wait till I was grown up some day. So I decided to follow them one night when they took off in their hunting flight. I found a road at the forest's edge and there decided to fulfill my pledge. While along that road I came, I thought to give myself a very good name. In case a member of that wonderful kingdom should pass by, he would know what a worthy prince was I. And if it should please him, just by chance, he might return me to my rightful inheritance!"

Castigio was impressed with the story. "Your Majesty, I shall take you there!" he exclaimed and bowed low on one knee. Almost immediately he thought, *What am I saying? I scarcely know the way back myself!* The words had seemed to pop out of his mouth before he even knew quite what he was saying. It was the very mention of that Star that had moved him so.

The cub was startled, "Are you a king?"

"Oh, no! But I was commissioned by the queen of Spain a long time ago to be a royal explorer, a conquistador!" said Castigio to make himself seem a little more worthy in the presence of a prince.

"Where is Spain?" asked Prince Zip scratching his head.

"It's a long way off. It doesn't really matter where it is, because I don't know how to get back."

"Do you know how to get to the Magical Kingdom of that Star?" asked Prince Zip doubtfully.

"No, not exactly, but I have been there, and it is just as you say!" As Castigio spoke he began to feel certain that he had not just dreamed it up because of the bump on his head after all. He was feeling bolder about the whole idea. The lion cub was staring at him with excitement, putting princely pride aside once more. He bounced up and down, nearly high enough to climb out of the hole.

"What did you see?" he landed at Castigio's feet and hugged them tight. "Tell me! Oh, please!"

Castigio was about to tell him when a blast of cool air whipped his face and something whizzed right past the two of them from behind, spinning like a top on

# Prince Zip

the ice. Castigio and Prince Zip stared in wonder as the thing came to a stop. It was Soot!

"My! My! My! Mercy sakes, my friend! You certainly do have a way of making introductions!" commented Castigio, remembering the way she had knocked him over in the road! "Meet Prince Zip!"

"I've met him already!" she snapped. "And he didn't act much like a prince to me!" she said as she teetered about in dizzy circles while trying hard to straighten herself from the spin.

Castigio was amazed at how stubbornly she had made up her mind, for she had not taken a liking to the cub at all. "Come on now, Soot. I'm surprised at you!"

"I don't like impersonators one bit!" she replied finally coming to a standstill. "First, it's a bee, and then it's a cat, and now it's a king? What next, naughty thing?" she demanded staring up at the cub.

"A prince," corrected Prince Zip apologetically.

"You see there! What did I tell you Castigio?! He's got another disguise and probably a million more! Can't trust the varmint! Worse than a wolf!" The lion cub sank down on all four paws and moved slowly behind the Spaniard as he eyed the snappy lamb with caution.

"But, Soot!" Castigio protested. "He truly is a Royal Highness, and we must try to help him find his inheritance. Why, he is lost too, just like us!"

Soot stared at the lion cub, trying to decide if all this were so. But she decided that it was really impossible to tell for sure. At last she said, "Castigio, you are to be trusted. A brave defender you are, so I will believe this to be as you say."

"Thank you, Soot!" Castigio sighed a little in relief, but Prince Zip kept a wary eye upon the lamb for the time being.

"Now tell me, Soot, how did you get down here with us? Are you stuck too?"

"No, I found another entrance. As I was digging it out to see if it would be big enough, I slipped on some loose gravel and slid all this way."

"Do you think we can crawl out then?" asked Prince Zip who was now very eager to get on his way to find the Kingdom.

Ignoring the lion cub, Soot said to Castigio, "We can all climb out one by one."

"Thank you again, Soot! Yet, I do not think that we can get on well together anywhere until we are all better friends." As Castigio was talking he got an idea, "Let us try an experiment, friends."

Soot and Zip watched with curiosity as Castigio moved about toward the entrance Soot had found, tapping the walls with his spear and listening now and then. They listened too. The lamb tilted her head, the lion cub closed his eyes, and Castigio cupped one hand behind his ear and raised up on his tiptoes.

"What are we listening for Castigio?" asked the lamb impatiently.

"Icicles!" he said.

"What?"

"Shh! It's for my experiment." Just then he rapped his spear against the ceiling of the cave and a soft tinkling, like the sound of a crystal bell, came floating back down to them. The sound was followed by a shower of shiny icicles, which fell in a string, all in a row.

"Ah, ha! I thought so!" exclaimed Castigio happily.

"Is that your experiment?" asked Prince Zip.

"No, these are just the parts I need. Come here, lion cub, Your Majesty, if you please."

Prince Zip obliged him, and Soot moved out of his way. Castigio bowed low, picking up the delicate string of icicles in both hands. He twisted them carefully into a circle and lifted them up to the lion cub's head. Nestling the icy crown into his golden locks of mane, he turned to Soot and joyfully proclaimed, "I present to you His Royal Highness, Prince Zip of the Kingdom of the Bright Morning Star and His Total Provinces!"

"Is that how it is to sound? It's wonderfully wonderful!" Prince Zip said as he suddenly felt very royal again.

"I suppose so, but what does it prove?" said the lamb hesitantly.

"Why, it proves he looks the part!" explained Castigio who was impressed with the results himself. "And that is as important as to say he is!"

Soot studied the cub again and concluded her inspection with a halfhearted agreement. It was not that she was not convinced, for even she had to admit

"I present to you His Royal Highness, Prince Zip."

in her heart of hearts that Prince Zip did indeed look rather noble. But she was actually jealous of their new companion and feared that Castigio might love her less.

"It will do for now," she said. Castigio's feelings were hurt, for he had meant to impress her and had been proud of his own success. But he decided not to let his disappointment show.

"Now what do you say we find our way out of here, friends?" he said trying to sound cheerful.

"I think the exit is behind you over there," Soot said as she tried to remember. But Castigio was standing in a different spot now. She wasn't sure because it was difficult to see in the dim light of the cave.

"No, I believe you spun past us from over there." The lion cub pointed in the opposite direction.

They all began walking in a circle and poking about, for none of them could bear to say that they were lost again. As they walked, Castigio felt a bit of dust hit his collar. Soot noticed a few pebbles sifting down from above in front of her, and Prince Zip heard a noise.

"Stop growling, Zip!" Soot said.

"I'm not doing any such thing!" said Prince Zip.

"What difference would it make if he were?" asked the Spaniard.

"He is disturbing my concentration!" fussed the lamb.

Then a grave voice agreed, "Mine too!"

Looking up, they all froze in their steps, for there, peering into the hole from above was a snarling, sneering black wolf!

"Yikes!" screamed Soot. "E-eek! It's Abaddon! Run for your lives!"

With that she started to run into the dark in the direction from which she thought she had come, knocking both the Spaniard and the lion cub to the ground. As she did, they all began to slide across the ice. They began to go faster and faster. Castigio ducked his head inside his helmet and covered his helmet with his arms as the three sped by slimy limestone walls. Without warning, they plunged down a chute into the lower levels of the cavern. It was as if someone had built a great sliding board for them to use in their escape.

Abaddon did not lose sight of them for an instant. The evil beast leaped into the hole and caught a glimpse of Soot's white fleece as it disappeared down the chute. There he stopped for a second to let his squinty red eyes adjust to the dark, for he was not worried about losing his prey. He was quite accustomed to this place and its many passageways.

The cave was his home!

# 6

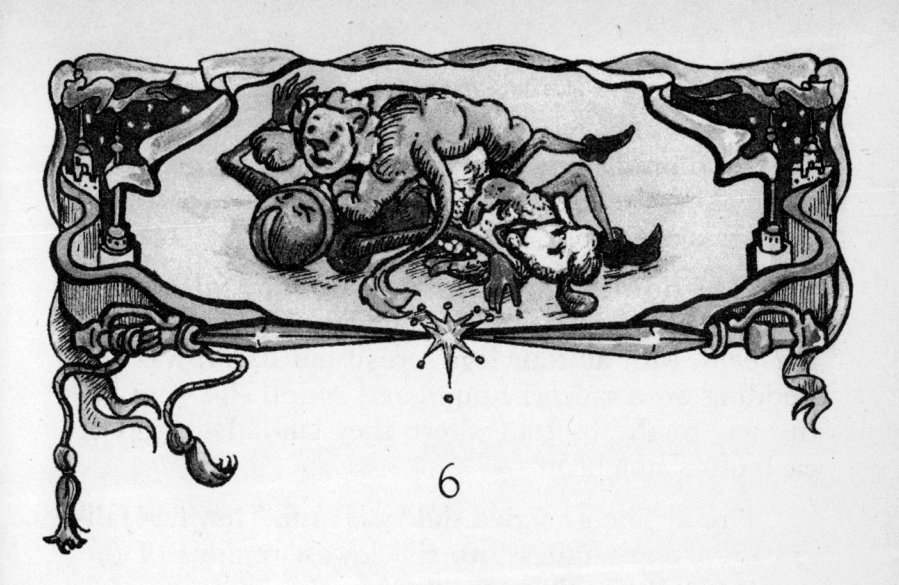

# A Prophecy

"**W**ee-ee! Hee-hee!" screamed Prince Zip, spinning and sliding down the icy chute on his back. He wasn't frightened a bit. The deeper into the cave the passageway twisted and turned, the more adventuresome he felt. The lion cub was enjoying the slide immensely as cold blasts of air whistled past his ears and bristled back his fur. "Wee-he!"

"Oh! Oh! Oh!" sputtered the Spaniard, for he was having quite a different time of it, spilling downward upside down, head first. Pit-tip! Zing-et-y dip! Bing! His helmet, as it banged along, barely stayed on his bald head. His shoulders jerked about roughly as his armor flipped up and down against the ice. Bump! Bump! Thump! Reaching out with his hands, he tried to stop himself, but found it impossible to grip anything along the cold slimy walls as he whizzed by them. "Mercy sakes alive!"

"My hoofs and curls! My hoofs and curls!" squealed the lamb, speeding ahead of them both on her belly, with all four legs spread out flat. It was like sledding on a saucer! Round and round she went, all the way to the bottom where they landed on top of each other in a heap!

Plunk! Their harried slide was over. They had fallen down many miles into the lowest regions of the cave, but none of them knew where they were.

"I shall never be the same again," moaned Castigio as he struggled to untangle himself from the others.

"Get your tail out of my face!" protested Soot as she brushed away furry orange fuzz from her nose and pushed with all her might against the cub who had landed smack dab on top of her. "Get up, I tell you!" she fussed again.

"Hold your breath! I'm trying!" Prince Zip assured her as he rolled over on his fat tummy, swishing his tail over her nose once more, and planting one paw in Castigio's face.

"Owe-ee!" the cub cried out as the impatient lamb bit his tail! She was not the least bit sorry, either, because he sprang into the air and left her free to scramble to her feet.

"Spth! Spth! I thought I'd die of suffocation!" exclaimed the lamb as she spit out balls of fur from her mouth.

A Prophecy

"Me too!" Castigio said as he sat up.

Prince Zip could not be bothered with either of them. His green eyes were as sharp as any cat's and began to adjust quickly to the darkness of the cave. Already he was busy exploring to see where their trip had brought them. But although even he could not see much in the blackness, he did not admit it. He was already planning a way to use the situation to play a prank upon the others.

"Sourpusses!" he mocked. "Open your eyes! Arise! Why this cave is absolutely magnificent!" He was lying. Actually he could see nothing.

"Of course it is magnificent," a sweet silky voice agreed.

They all looked up to try to see from where the voice had come. Castigio and Soot squinted in the darkness, but it was as black as black could be. Castigio felt about for his spear, but could not find it.

"Who said that?" whispered Soot.

"An angel and not a spook, I hope!" Castigio whispered back. "Did we die and slide below? Pinch me to see if I'm alive."

"You are quite alive my dear," the soft soothing voice assured him.

"Castigio, what sort of beast is it?" Soot asked, trembling like a leaf in the frosty cave. Castigio hadn't the faintest idea, but he hated to seem unwise when Soot was counting on him so. "The regular kind," he whispered in a comforting tone.

"Where are we? Do you happen to know?" called the lion cub as he circled about trying to catch sight of

93

the source of the voice. This sort of thing rarely frightened him as his curiosity always got the best of him first.

"For heaven sakes, Your Majesty, don't agitate it!" Castigio begged. We are very rude to intrude upon it this way in the first place! Leave it alone. Oh, let's! It may well forget us in a moment or two and go away." He hoped with all his heart that the thing could not see him any better than he could see it, which was not at all. The hair on his neck was standing straight up and he had the most eerie feeling of being watched. He was certain his hopes were vain when again the voice spoke directly to them.

"You are at the center of many concourses," said the lovely voice.

"What's a concourse?" whispered Soot dreading the worst.

"Shhh!" said Castigio trying hard to concentrate so that he might decide whether the beast was friend or foe. Its voice was having a soothing effect on his senses making him nervous about beginning to feel so calm.

"Do not be afraid. I won't hurt you, Castigio, nor your little lamb or your brave prince."

They were all shocked that it knew their names.

"You are in the center of my palace. I knew you would come. There are many avenues leading here. Your passage may have been rough, but other paths are worse. Are you all intact? No bruises or broken bones, I hope?" Soot was relieved to know that at least it was a caring creature.

# A Prophecy

"We are all just fine!" quipped the lion cub.

"Good! I believed you would be, but still, others sometimes arrive here in much worse shape. It is such a pity!" said the kind voice sympathetically.

"What others?" they all asked in one voice.

"Travelers and weary beasts, victims of the same evil creature who chased you in here."

"Abaddon!" breathed the lamb.

"Yes, Soot, but would you be so kind as not to mention his name in my presence again. It has such an ugly sound." The lamb blushed in embarrassment.

"No need to be so wounded, my dear. It is just a rule of manners in my palace. Now, where was I? Oh, yes. I always know when folks are going to drop in, and it is a wonderful chance to help them."

"How?" asked Castigio who was very interested in getting out of that dark place as soon as possible.

"Well, there is always a reason for their visits even though neither they nor the enemy knows it.

"They come from many walks of life up there. Some of them walk with their noses so high in the air that they never see the holes and traps that the evil creature has dug for them to fall into. Others fall through an opening in the earth because of some jealous rascal who has led them there to do them in. Still others are murderers hiding in the caves from honest men who pursue them. Then there are thieves who sneak into the caves to rob my treasures. Most of them are not much more worthy than the wolf. But I must try to help them all. It is my duty and the desire of the one whom I serve here.

"Because the travelers are caught off guard when they are attacked and pushed through one of the holes, it is my task to guard this spot and greet them when they arrive here. If I can, I try to redirect them before it is too late."

Castigio, Soot, and Prince Zip remembered how they had been fighting before their fall.

"Too late?" quivered the lamb.

"Yes. If they dillydally here too long, the wolf will finish them off. And if their pride or evil ways prevent them from following my advice on their way out, then the end is just the same."

"Ooh!" gasped the three huddling together, as they began to wonder what would become of them.

"Will I ever see my Shepherd?" sobbed Soot.

"Will I never see my magic kingdom?" pouted Prince Zip.

Castigio said nothing for he was petrified with fright.

"Stop your whining!" scolded the beast. "You are here for a very good reason, the best of all reasons why anyone has yet come my way. Your visit is no mistake. Now hush up! Listen! I have much to tell you!" Even though the voice was scolding them, it was soothing and would have lulled them to sleep had it not suddenly paused.

The cavern was so quiet that Castigio could hear the lion cub purring and the little lamb breathing. Except for the sound of dripping water all around, there was a mysterious stillness. Nothing stirred down there deep in that cave. The moments seemed like

A Prophecy

hours to Castigio. At last he nervously called out in a crackling voice, "Are you still there?"

"Yes," came the reply. "But you should not have spoken out for I was listening."

"To what?" asked Prince Zip.

"Never mind. Let's just get on with the business at hand."

"It would certainly help if we could see you," said the impatient lamb.

"Yes, but perhaps that is not wise."

They wondered why not, but dared not say another thing for fear of interrupting again. More silence followed.

It spoke at last. "I suppose we are safe. Let me see what I can do."

They all heard the sound of sighing and the tinkling of icicles falling from a great height as the beast moved. It seemed to move a wide distance around them. Castigio twitched his mustache nervously.

"Look up here. Can you see me now?" it said sweetly.

Castigio rubbed his eyes hard and noticed how they watered, for staring into the blackness of the cave had made them sore. It was not easy for him to take in the lovely sight at first. But little by little his eyes adjusted to focus upon a soft glowing object high above his head.

"Oh, yes! We can see you!" they exclaimed as they saw light.

There built into a ledge was the seat of a magnificent throne, shimmering with icicles and gigantic stalagmites and stalactites that encircled it from the ceiling of the cavern to the floor. The throne was more than twice the size of any that could be thought up.

A canopy of velvety green moss stretched across the ceiling and hung as drapery along the entire length of each side. Nuggets of unmined gold glistened as they protruded from frozen columns of ice lining the walls. Glittering sapphires of the bluest hue sparkled like mosaic tiles along the floor. Hundreds of glowworms inched along and thousands of tiny fish darted about in sculptured pools covered by a thin cap of ice at the base of the great throne.

Millions of strange tiny creatures sat or perched in nests built in the hanging moss and crevices of the wall behind. They were singing in high clear pitches. But none of the three travelers recognized the languages of their songs. The melody sounded much like the chittering of birds on a spring day.

Seated in the midst of it all was the most gigantic cheetah that any of them had ever seen.

"She's a cat like me!" sighed Prince Zip in amazement. Neither Castigio nor Soot heard him because they were too enthralled taking in the sight.

The cheetah was completely blue – her spots were blue and so were her eyes. Tiny spots of many sizes seemed to change places on her skin, not staying in the same place for an instant. Each paw was as big as a full grown man, which made Castigio feel as small as a dwarf. She would have seemed truly terrible if her voice had not been so soft and sweet.

"Could you turn down the lights?" asked the lamb bravely. "Why, you are so wonderful that I can't bear to look at you!"

"No," answered the cheetah. "Once you have asked to see, I have no control over your not seeing me."

"Why do you live down here in this dark place where so few can ever see your beauty and grace?" asked Prince Zip who was very conscious of such vain things.

"To begin with, this is not a dark place. I could see you perfectly from the moment you arrived," she said.

"Why couldn't we see too?" asked Castigio doubtfully.

"It was possible, Castigio. Especially for you," she said, curling up on her couchlike throne.

"What do you mean?" asked the Spaniard, puzzled.

"Only those with a thirst for truth and light can see through the deepest darkness, even seeing through the void of sleep where only dreams bring light and hope," she said.

"But I could see nothing, not even my hand in front of my face!" he protested. "Now we see you up there only because of something you did. I don't even know what that might have been."

"Not true. You are not seeing me because of something I did," she corrected him gently. Castigio was amazed at how such a gentle spirit could inhabit such an enormous body. "It was something you said that changed your sight," she explained. "Look around you. To you, the rest of the cavern will appear just as dark as before."

Castigio slowly turned in a circle. Indeed only the throne where Blue Cheetah lay was lit. All else was still enveloped in a creepy darkness that made him feel ill at ease again. "I don't understand," he muttered to himself and then jumped half out of his suit of armor when Blue Cheetah spoke again as if she had been able to read his thoughts.

"Of course you don't understand, do you? All of you can see me now simply because you asked."

"I don't believe it!" said Prince Zip stoutly. "It's just a trick!"

"No, it's not, my dear," replied the cheetah calmly. "Castigio, do you believe me?"

He did not like to be put on the spot like that, but said, "I suppose so. Why would you lie?" He also didn't want to anger the great creature lest it suddenly change disposition and pounce on him.

"I am not a chameleon, Castigio. I do not lie!" She knew his thoughts again! "I will show you. Is there something else you desire to see? Perhaps something brighter than me?"

"Oh, yes! The sun, the sun!" cried the lamb who longed for her pasture where she could play again in the light of day. It seemed a far ways away.

"You shall see it soon enough, but there is no need for the sun here," said Blue Cheetah. "Castigio, have you forgotten the sight that first welcomed you to this island? Can't you remember how it beckoned you to the mountains in the night? How it led you and guided you there?"

"The Morning Star!" he gasped. How could she have known about that? How did she know everything else? "I thought...I thought...I...," stammered Castigio.

"...it was just a dream?" Blue Cheetah said in a sweet knowing way.

"Why, yes. Have you seen it too?" He was almost afraid to ask.

"Would you like to see it again?" she coaxed him.

"Certainly. Oh, mercy sakes, yes!" exclaimed Castigio full of wonder. So! He was not an old fool after all as El Capitan had said. The Star really did exist. And he suspected that the Magical Kingdom and the Fountain of Youth did too! Castigio was overwhelmed with joy at the very thought of seeing the Star again, for he had felt so alone since that night.

"Then close your eyes and say so aloud!" Blue Cheetah told him. Soot and Prince Zip stood next to Castigio in wonder. They decided to try what Castigio was doing too. They squinted their eyes tightly shut. Just as Castigio was about to open his mouth, they heard a terrible snarling noise behind them.

"Yikes, the wolf!" shrieked the lamb.

It was Abaddon. He had found them at last. He came whizzing down the same slippery path upon which they had entered. Seeing the lamb standing there had given him evil delight. He had let out a horrifying growl as he approached them, meaning to carry off Soot to a terrible feast. But once he hit the right past them totally out of control. As he slid by the lamb, he thrust out a claw to snatch her, but missed, only grabbing at air. Abaddon's plans to gobble up the lamb were ruined!

Soot nearly fainted on Castigio's shoe. He caught her as she fell there, trembling with fright. Castigio fumbled about for his spear. Even Prince Zip bounced to her rescue, gnashing his small white teeth as fiercely as he could manage.

With an ear splitting "Cra-a-ack!" Abaddon crashed into the base of Blue Cheetah's throne. He did not recognize the throne, because his ears were ringing and his head was reeling as he staggered up onto his hind feet. His clumsy entrance had made him all the more angry and vicious. As soon as he was able, he hunched his back and took aim to leap upon the three.

But in that instant, a great blue paw whacked him on the hind quarters. In shock he bit his tongue and, with a look of surprise on his face, went sprawling across the ice in front of them again. As Castigio and his companions stood watching in disbelief, Abaddon disappeared from sight howling in pain! At the high speed he was traveling down the frozen river of ice, it was certain that the three would not be bothered with him for a while. His journey would end many, many miles away!

"Unusual luck!" remarked Castigio.

"It was bound to happen," Blue Cheetah said softly. She seemed unbothered by the whole affair.

"That is why I was waiting to see if it was wise to shine light on this place. He was sure to see you if I did. Some things are better left alone until the proper

Abaddon crashed into the base of
Blue Cheetah's throne.

time. However, the Morning Star was here and seemed willing to lighten your eyes. So I was certain that all would turn out well as indeed it has...don't you think so, Castigio?"

Castigio did not hear much of what the cheetah said. He stood there stunned by what appeared over her head in the instant she began to speak. There above her throne was the blazing Morning Star, spotless and brilliant as any sun. He was mesmerized by it and could not understand how it was that his eyes could stare right into the face of it and behold such glory without being blinded. "Magnificent, magnificent!" he mumbled to himself many times over as he stood there gawking.

"What's he saying?" Soot asked Prince Zip. But the cub ignored her too and seemed as much in another world as did Castigio. She watched in puzzlement as the springy cub leaped from beside her and bounced off into the darkness. She could hear him exclaiming, "Wee-ee Hee! Hee!" as he ricocheted off the walls.

Prince Zip was having the time of his young life. He could not see the Bright Morning Star as Castigio did, but its presence there affected him too. As he had stood watching the cheetah speak, the cavern had been lit up for him. Its immensity and enormous sculptures of stalactites and stalagmites awaited him with endless possibilities for exploration and games of hide and seek. Each piece of rock was striped with minerals shining with every color of the rainbow, and covered with layers of ice that made them a dazzling sparkling forest of stone. It was more than anyone could hope to discover in a lifetime.

# A Prophecy

Prince Zip was getting ready to explore another passageway when Blue Cheetah called him back. She knew he would eventually wander outside the realm of the Star's bright rays and become lost in the blackness of the cave again. He heard her call and stopped long enough to listen, but did not intend to obey. Again he heard her voice echoing. It seemed to have such authority and power over him. He dared not resist. Reluctantly he returned to Soot's side.

"Where were you? Weren't you afraid of getting lost, you silly thing?" demanded Soot.

"What do you mean lost? This cave is full of richer gems than diamonds cost, and the most wonderful places to have races. On the river of ice you can slide! And in the nooks and crannies hide! It's a great place to play! I could stay here all day!"

"Well, I can't see a thing more than the cheetah's throne, Castigio mumbling like a ninny, and you acting as if you've lost your senses!" she said very confused. "What's happened to you two? Did you see the wolf? He almost killed me! Don't you think we ought to ask that big cat up there how to leave?"

"Yes! I saw him," Prince Zip said. "She gave him what he deserved all right, the varmint! Didn't you see the marvelous way this whole place lit up when she whacked him? Why...we're standing in it right now!"

"No! No! I can't see a thing!" Soot cried, "I think he scared you silly!"

Blue Cheetah decided that it was time to put an end to their dispute and spoke up again. "Each of you has seen a different vision in this place, my dear ones. None of you are the same.

"This is not by accident, because the Morning Star has been guiding your way from the first day you were lost. It was certain that the wolf would chase all of you here in time. We waited to see how you would come together. The measure of your interest in your own destiny and that of others will determine how often you will be able to see the face of this Star. I have nothing to do with this. He is the source of light in this place, and only he causes me to know these things as we keep company here.

"Castigio has the desire to see eternal things and to know great peace and glory such as he has never had but has always dreamed of since the days of his youth. Therefore, he has eyes to see such beauty. And the Morning Star has chosen from time to time to reveal himself to him, because Castigio will believe in the end."

Prince Zip was listening intently at the mention of the Star. The mere mention of it had reminded him of the maiden's song in the forest, for she had spoken of it too.

"Prince Zip, indeed you are a royal heir as you call yourself, my dear," Blue Cheetah said. "But your pride blinds you to many things. You must learn to think more of others if you wish not to travel alone on your journey to the Kingdom. A king is not meant to rule for his own pleasure, but for the welfare of his subjects. If you do not learn this lesson, then you are destined to fail outside its very gates before you enter in.

"You believe in the Star because you have heard of it, but have not seen it. Its guiding light is enough for you. You have journeyed this far in hope, the hope

## A Prophecy

of finding its Kingdom. But the Kingdom is not the power or the prize. What lies within and who enters with you is far more important. Thus, my dear, you are not ready to see the Star's bright face. But one day you will yearn to. When it opens its light to you, as on this day, be quick to see what you must do."

"Does the Morning Star speak so that I will know where to seek for it?" asked Prince Zip, trying to understand the strange prophecy.

"It doesn't need a voice to do its work, for it accomplishes all things well," answered Blue Cheetah. "There are many such as I who are willing to speak its thoughts. Our task is to learn to watch his motions as a servant keeps his eye on his master's signals to know his bidding. In time Prince Zip, you will be a watcher too."

The lion cub was greatly encouraged that he would find his destiny now.

"But what about me?" sobbed Soot, blinking back the tears that rolled down her cheeks. She was feeling left out. She had not seen Castigio's marvelous Star and knew she was not a blue-blood as Prince Zip had claimed. "What is left for me?" she bleated.

"Much, my dear, for your heart is tender and your ways are simple," Blue Cheetah said. "You are eager to believe good in those that need your courage. It is only your tongue that causes you to trip yourself and be faint-hearted. Take courage, little lamb. Know that there will be those to see you home into the arms of your Shepherd."

"My Shepherd!" she swooned at the thought of him, because he was a caring fellow to be admired.

107

"He is out looking for you this very hour," Blue Cheetah said. "He is most like the Morning Star than anyone else I know, and his home is in the Star's distant Kingdom. That is where he was leading the flock when the spring lambs were born. You are just as surely meant to reach that Kingdom as any of your companions!"

"Then why can't I see his Star?" begged the lamb.

"You must see it through the eye of faith, my dear Soot, and by those who dream of eternal things that last. Do you think of such things?"

"Why, no, not really," admitted the lamb. "I only miss my mother and the Shepherd and the flock."

"Very well then, one day you will meet him at the gates of his Kingdom and your desires will change. Until then, my dear, you must follow Castigio, who sees such things, and you will arrive there safely," she said.

"Oh, gladly!" sighed the lamb, "He is such a brave friend already!"

"Now listen carefully, all of you," Blue Cheetah said, looking around at them one by one. "Castigio, my dear, you too please," she added because he was not listening. He still stood beside her throne in a trance, staring up at the Bright Morning Star. "Very well then, my dear," she said to herself. "If I must, then so I must!"

Soot and Prince Zip listened wonderingly as her voice trailed off to a whisper, and she began to stretch her enormous back while she gracefully got up from the couchlike throne. As she did, the light of the

A Prophecy

Morning Star began to quickly fade. And its glorious light transferred itself onto the spots of her skin.

The surface of her sleek coat began to sparkle as her blue spots seemed to shift positions. It looked very much like the surface of a pool of water, glittering in the sunlight on a summer's day. And as she moved from the throne's high ledge to the floor below, her body stretching downward, paws first and tail last, she looked very much like a refreshing blue waterfall cascading over the icy pillars of limestone. A melodic sound, very similar to that of a bubbling brook, could be heard in the cave as she descended, and ceased as soon as her body became still again.

Castigio, Soot and Prince Zip stood speechless as they watched the fantastic creature. Castigio thought that he had heard that same waterfall sound somewhere before, perhaps in the Kingdom. He was not quite sure. At last Soot broke their silence, "How did she do that?"

"Never mind, my dear," Blue Cheetah answered her as she settled down, tucking her paws beneath her. "I must decide what instruction to give you as the time is drawing nigh for you to be on your way." Then she paused thoughtfully and added, "You haven't eaten today have you?"

"Berries we have!" said Castigio, feeling very naked in his underdrawers as he reminded himself of the whole affair.

"We shall replace your bloomers and stockings, Castigio. But first you must eat. I cannot send my visitors away so hungry. Please come this way, will you?" she invited them. Blue Cheetah rose up and began to move as fluid as water again.

109

The three travelers felt strange, as if they were floating along behind her. Castigio looked down at his feet to be sure they were still walking on the icy cavern floor. Indeed they were not. Instead he found that each of them was standing on a raft that was being towed by a golden harness strapped to a wreath of semi-precious gems around Blue Cheetah's head. Only the top of her head and the tip of her nose were visible as she swam through a river of blue sparkling water. In front of her was a frozen channel of ice that may have once been an underground stream. But it melted into a rushing river as she touched it. Blue Cheetah said nothing as she continued to swim a great distance through the winding passageway cut into the cavern by a river thousands of years ago. Castigio and his companions rode along in silence. They were not sure what might happen next. They hugged each other tight and waited to see where she was taking them.

At last they came to a great opening in the cavern. It was larger than the ballroom of any palace. It was filled with a thick mist about knee deep. Scurrying around inside were many little creatures and animals of every kind. They were busy carrying large, elaborately carved silver trays loaded with wonderful smelling delicacies, fruits and splendid desserts.

In the center of the room was a golden table draped with pure white linen reaching to the floor. The table was set with goblets and plates of ornate fashion and lined with enough chairs to feed a king's army. One could not see the end of it no matter how he might strain his eyes.

Entertainment was provided as well. A melodic tune was filling the chamber from the strings of many

Only the top of the cheetah's head and the tip of her
nose were visible as she swam.

golden harps, each playing by themselves as they lined the walls all around. The melody seemed to invite one's feet to dance.

Castigio was having great difficulty controlling his legs. They insisted on following the tempting music as he disembarked from the raft. Prince Zip and Soot were already trailing behind Blue Cheetah as she made her way to the table.

"That's what I like! A feast fit for a king!" exclaimed the lion cub, patting his tummy.

"For many kings, my dear," corrected Blue Cheetah.

Prince Zip immediately saw that his pride was showing, for he had mistakenly assumed right off that they had landed in his kingdom already.

"Welcome to the great dining hall of the Bright Morning Star and his army!" beckoned Blue Cheetah. "Eat your fill. But be polite. I shall speak with you in a little while. Time is running short. We must hurry. Now come!"

Each grabbed a seat and was soon waited on by ferrets, in red tuxedo tails and white cummerbunds with shiny gold buttons. The ferrets did not speak a word but busied themselves filling the guests' drinks and placing more food before them than they had ever seen before.

Soot stood on her chair with her front hoofs on top of the table and nibbled at grapes, raisins and a heaping platter of other fruits.

The cub sat up smartly just like a little prince and gobbled down unusual meat pies and tasty pastries.

Each grabbed a seat and was soon waited on by ferrets.

Castigio removed his helmet and loaded it with fruit. Then he thought better of it for being rude and emptied it back out again. The smooth silverware fit nicely in his gnarled old hands. He had never touched such luxury. He felt very fine indeed. His delight was to sample everything upon the table. He was grateful.

Blue Cheetah took her leave and reclined among the golden harps to watch over them. When she thought they had eaten enough, lest any of them burst, she called for their attention and proceeded with her instructions for the journey that lay ahead.

"Castigio, I must warn you, my dear. The way out of here is not an easy climb. The mountains that lie between this place and the Kingdom are treacherous to cross. No man from this island has ever survived the trip through them. None of them will dare to dream that they can."

"Am I the only one to ever see it?" he asked.

"No. There are soldiers that defend it and some who have seen it, but when they reach here they are in worse shape than you and, well...." Her voice trailed off into a sorrowful sigh.

"You mean the wolf? You mean they...you mean...?" Castigio could not bear to say what he was thinking, because he felt fear begin to creep up both ankles and wrap around his knocking knees.

"Yes, my dear," she said. "We needn't discuss the grizzly details. Braver men have tried to enter the gates and failed. None were humble enough to allow their dreams to guide them. The Morning Star sent them plenty of dreams, but they devised their own routes and failed."

A Prophecy

"I believe in dreams!" said Castigio, quickly hoping to save his name from that list.

"Yes, and so you have a better chance. But all is not certain. See that you follow them as best you can." Blue Cheetah said wisely. "It will be important to the others you meet along the way."

"But I am not a brave man!" protested Castigio looking into her huge face. As soon as he said this, Blue Cheetah's brows knit together and her nose wrinkled back in a terrifying frown. Castigio was sure she would not harm him. But instantly he knew his words had wounded her. "I'm sorry. I will do my best," he vowed. She did not say another word, but seemed pleased.

"Tell him how to get us out of here!" interrupted the lamb when she at last had her chance.

"Very well. Yes, it is time to get on with the journey," replied Blue Cheetah kindly. "You must take a route no others have taken, because I am sending you to visit a friend of mine. He is a pilgrim who has traveled much of the way to the Kingdom and back. He will tell you where to go from there, if you remind him that I sent you. He owes me the favor. He has a weapon that he borrowed from me many years ago. Since I happen to know he is not using it, tell him that I said for him to give it to you."

"What is it?" interrupted Castigio.

"It has great power over the enemies you will meet in the mountains. You must not be lazy about learning to use it. You may need it when you least expect!"

Castigio did not like to hear of such trials, but dared not argue the point as before. Soot was not concerned with the details. She was anxious to get on with the plans for escape. "So where do we find this pilgrim?" she begged.

"Crawl under the legs of the chair at the head of the table and kick the floor three times," Blue Cheetah said. "A ferret will let you through a secret trapdoor, which the wolf has never seen. In case he comes back, he will know nothing of it. No one has used this tunnel for eons and ages. But I do believe you will find it passable. Take nothing with you, not even your spear, Castigio," she commanded. Obediently he dropped it and knotted his worried empty hands together.

"How long will it take?" asked Prince Zip curiously.

"As long as it does," Blue Cheetah replied flatly.

"When you get to the end of the tunnel you will meet the pilgrim. He is just your size, I do believe Castigio, and I am sure he will be happy to lend you a change of bloomers and stockings."

"Oh, splendid!" sighed the Spaniard. He was relieved that he would not have to go through life without them.

"Hurry, now. Be off with you!" said Blue Cheetah in her silky voice.

They were glad to be on their way and ran to the chair to exit as quickly as possible, almost forgetting their manners. "She was a wonderful cat, wasn't she?" remarked Prince Zip feeling proud to be kin somehow

# A Prophecy

as they rounded the corner of the well-spread table once more. "Oh, yes, but we forgot to thank her!" remembered the lamb whose belly was pleasantly stuffed. Turning to thank her, they were surprised to see she had vanished.

Castigio hurried and climbed beneath the chair as she had said to do. He kicked the floor three times. On the third try he heard Blue Cheetah's voice once more behind him, "If you need help, my dear, call on the Morning Star wherever you are!" He would have looked to see where she was, but had not a second's notice before the trapdoor in the floor gave way beneath his feet. Down he dropped into the tunnel. Prince Zip was next to jump in. Soot came scurrying after, not wishing to be left behind again.

A ferret greeted them just as Blue Cheetah had promised. He handed Castigio a small glass vial full of glowworms. He said not a word, then scampered back up the hole. The trapdoor slammed shut behind him with a thud, and darkness settled in around them once more. Castigio held up the tiny vial of glowworms to light their path and saw that the tunnel ran before and behind them. Which way should they go?

# 7

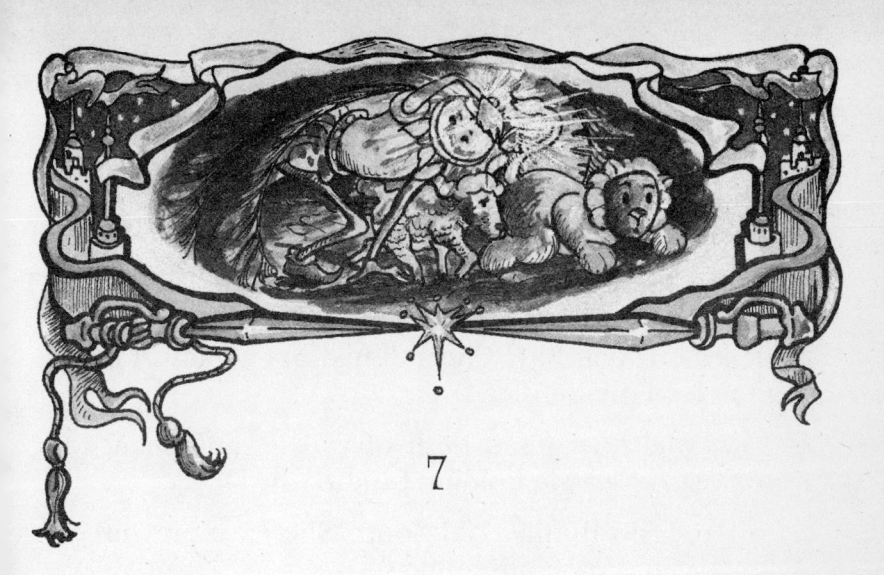

# Trapped!

**N**arrow spaces made Castigio feel claustrophobic. To him claustrophobia was worse than seasickness. His head spun dizzily. He felt he could not breath as he stood beneath the trapdoor in the tunnel.

Light from the glowworms revealed that the passage was not very high at all. Castigio soon suspected that no one taller than an oversized ferret had ever used it. The sides were rugged and appeared to have been hewn out of limestone, possibly by a small animal using his claws. Standing there, bent halfway over like a hunchback, Castigio wondered if the tunnel would end up wider or smaller. "Oh, my, things do seem to become worse and worse down here!" he sighed.

"Don't say things like that, Castigio!" scolded the lamb nervously. "Just get us out of here. Blue Cheetah said you could," she added hopefully.

"Yes, brave leader, get to walking, won't you? It's certain to be a long way up!" urged Prince Zip, only a little jealous that Blue Cheetah had not commissioned him to lead them instead.

"Oh, do be quiet, both of you. I can't seem to think," said Castigio holding his dizzy head.

"Well, do think!" said Soot. "She gave our directions to you. I wasn't listening."

"She gave them to us all," insisted Prince Zip. "The responsibility on each for himself must fall! Who needs a leader anyway?"

"I do!" cried the lamb.

"No, you don't. All we have to do is find which way is up and head in that direction," argued the lion cub. Then he took a few steps to the right and found that the tunnel floor tilted slightly up. He bounded back to the lamb and darted off to the left only to find there was a steep incline there as well. "We're lost again," he said at last.

"No, we're not!" contradicted the lamb, "Blue Cheetah said this was a sure way out!"

"Then we have to find the right direction. I'll look again. But I have to see further than this," said Prince Zip, leaping up at the vial of glowworms which Castigio held tightly in his hand. "Give me that!" the cub said as he grabbed for the vial.

But Castigio moved his hand just in the nick of time, for the careless cub would surely have knocked

# Trapped!

the vial to the ground. "Not on your life! Get your clumsy mitts away!" exclaimed Castigio, hugging the vial to his chest.

"Oh, be still!" squealed the lamb frantically. She did not see where there was any room for wrestling in that small space. "Stop it! Won't you? Why don't you see? We're fighting just like all those others who failed before us. If we give in to our own feelings, we'll never get away. Blue Cheetah warned us. Didn't she?"

"Soot, you are right!" said Castigio sinking down upon the ground. He found that having a little space above him made him feel more normal. "We've got to put our heads together on this and think a minute. It's certain there must be an easy way out, or she would have given us a clear sign to search for. Let us think."

Castigio ducked into the peace and quiet of his familiar thinking space, his trusty helmet. Prince Zip stubbornly obeyed. Soot squinted her eyes and put her head between her hoofs.

Inside his helmet Castigio began to ask himself this question, "Which way is right?"

The impish echo had not been used in a while but it was ready. "Right is the way," it replied.

Castigio liked its familiar sound. "More light is what we need," he said.

"We need more light," said the echo obligingly. "A light that is bright!" said Castigio.

"Bright is that light!" said the echo.

"What light?" asked Castigio.

"Light what?" answered the echo.

"Well, the path!" said Castigio very matter-of-factly.

"The path well!" said the echo.

"How?" thought Castigio aloud.

"Wow! WOW! Wow!" carried on the echo. It had reached its annoying stage as usual again. So Castigio took the helmet back off to sift through the thoughts on his own.

"What lights our path?" he asked aloud.

"Glowworms!" said Prince Zip. Castigio was a little startled because he wasn't expecting the echo to reply and had momentarily forgotten about the others. The answer was, however, just the right one, for it suddenly triggered an idea in his head.

"That's it, my friend!" Castigio exclaimed jumping up on his feet. He forgot about the low ceiling of the tunnel and promptly bumped his head. "Ouch!"

"What is it?" begged the other two.

"I have an idea, and a headache too!" he grumbled.

"Hurry! Tell us!" they urged.

"It's the glowworms! That was Blue Cheetah's final gift to us. They are used to her kingdom of light. Perhaps if we turn one loose it will crawl toward the daylight and lead us out of here!"

"I don't think that will work!" said the lion cub. "It may just crawl home. Then we'll be right back in the throne room."

"Well, I think it's a stroke of genius if you care for my opinion, Castigio," commented Soot supportively.

# Trapped!

"Even if we end up there, it will be better than here, and we could ask Blue Cheetah for better directions. I say let's try it!"

Castigio stooped down on his hands and knees. Carefully, he opened the top of the vial and tilted it over so that only one tiny worm could crawl out. Soot stuck her nose down low to watch it, but Prince Zip only crossed his arms over his chest, tapped his foot and huffed indignantly.

The worm was a florescent pink, a very delicate thing. It wriggled over the edge of the vial with its many miniature feet, until it reached the tunnel floor. Pausing a second, it looked right into their faces, as if to be sure they were watching, then took off with incredible speed toward the right side of the passage and disappeared up the steep incline.

"Tickle my whiskers! I didn't know those things could move so fast!" exclaimed the Spaniard.

"Come on! Let's follow it!" yelled Soot as she trotted up the tunnel after it. Castigio and Prince Zip came scrambling after her, seeing by the rest of the glowworms' light. Catching up with her at last, they found Soot standing alone with a woeful expression on her face. "Where's the glowworm Lambkin?" Castigio asked. "No telling by now. It was out of sight before I knew it! Gone!" wept the lamb.

"Never mind Soot. At least it showed us the direction we need to travel. We'll find the way out. Don't be a worry wart." Castigio said, putting a comforting arm around her. "It will be all right. You'll see," he said, and hoped so, as he led the way.

The worm wriggled over the edge of the vial
with its many miniature feet.

Crawling up the many miles of tunnel was hard work for all of them, especially Castigio. His claustrophobia was bothering him all the more, and he did not fit as well as the other two because he was taller. At times the path seemed almost impossible to pass through, and he had to slither sideways like a snake, using his limbs like a spider between slabs of rock. He was forever bumping his head. It seemed as if they would never reach the end of the tunnel. None of them knew whether it was day or night and time to sleep, but they all had grown very tired.

"We must rest here!" said Soot in a weary, breathless voice. "I can't force myself to go a step farther until we do."

"Me either," said the roly-poly lion cub who was beginning to regret having gorged his tummy so full at the feast. His gluttony had made it nearly impossible to squeeze through the tighter places. Once, along the way he had gotten stuck, and Castigio had to pull on his mane hard, while Soot bit his tail from the other side as incentive to move. That experience demolished his ego, and he was quite worn out.

"Very well then!" agreed the Spaniard. And they all nestled down in a cozy pile for a nap.

Not long afterward, they were awakened by the clatter of pebbles raining down upon them from the ceiling. At first it was only a few, but then it became a regular downpour! Scratching and grunting noises accompanied the falling pebbles until finally the fuzzy head of a mole popped through the wall.

"Who are you?" they all said, shaking dust and pebbles from themselves, in surprise.

"Who goes there?" sputtered the mole squinting in the pink light of the glowworms. "What do you think you're doing in my tunnel?"

"Your tunnel?" asked Prince Zip in defense. "We have every right to be here!"

"Blue Cheetah sent us this way!" added Soot.

"Blue Who?" the mole asked as it continued to push its way through.

"Blue Cheetah! She rules this cavern. Don't you know?" offered Castigio.

"Boo who? Blue you!" said the mole sarcastically. "Never heard of it. Doesn't matter who. Just get out of my way! I'm coming through!" and he did.

A large part of the wall caved in all around the creature and knocked the vial right out of Castigio's hand. He juggled it with first one hand and then the other, finally managing to catch it an inch above the ground.

"Whew! That was close!" Castigio gasped. "You should be more careful with others' belongings. Why, just think if you had broken that! We'd all be in the dark right now and could not make proper introductions." Soot shivered at the very thought of being in the pitch-black dark again.

"I'm not interested in introductions. I haven't any time for it!" the mole said. "Besides, there is nothing wrong with being in the dark, is there? You ought to try it sometime. It is the most natural thing to do!" crabbed the mole as it scaled the other wall and began to dig a second hole.

"Blue Who?" the mole asked.

"Why, you're blind, aren't you?" Castigio said as he realized that the mole had to feel his way around with every step he took.

"What's that?" it asked sincerely as it tunneled out of sight. With a last flip of its hind paw, it set off an avalanche. The three watched in horror as the vial of glowworms was jarred out of Castigio's hands. Dirt and pebbles buried it, closing in the small passageway where they had planned to go.

"It's dark! It's dark!" sobbed Soot in a terrified instant as she struggled to see. "Don't panic!" yelled Castigio. "Blue Cheetah said we would get through, and somehow we will!"

"How do you know?" cried Prince Zip.

"I just know," Castigio said. "The Morning Star will surely help us if we ask to see it."

"That didn't work for me," Prince Zip doubted. "But you might as well give it a try. What is there to lose?"

Castigio was afraid to try on his own, so he said, "Let's be wise first. Maybe we can do what it would have us do on our own. I hate to bother it again."

"Then what would you suggest?" asked the cub.

"Let me see," said Soot. "That mole came down upon us from above our heads. That means he started near the surface I bet. Perhaps he has dug other tunnels wider than this one. If we can just feel around and find the way he came in, then we can crawl out."

"Impossible!" said Prince Zip, trying to find his paws in the dark.

## Trapped!

"The mole did it, didn't he? And he was blind." Castigio reminded him as he stood up and began to run his hands along the wall above his head. "Ah, ha!" he exclaimed at last. "I found it! A hole! Another tunnel!"

"Can we fit?" asked the cub.

"We shall have to try," Castigio resolved.

"Who shall be first?" asked Soot and Prince Zip together. Normally Prince Zip would have taken on the adventure. But he was feeling so fat that he did not relish the idea of getting stuck again. "It will have to be you, Castigio!" he said sadly.

Castigio did not like the idea, but he knew by now it was expected of him. "All right. Give me a push up there and be sure to follow soon!" he said.

Soot offered her back as a footstool. Castigio climbed up. "I can feel cool air blowing on my face up here, but I'm not high enough to hoist myself through this hole. See if you can push me higher, Soot."

The little lamb took a deep breath and pushed up her back with all of her might. Castigio grabbed at the hole to catch hold but missed. At the same time Soot's legs gave way from under her, and she landed flat on her belly.

"You're squishing me!" she squealed.

"Oh, dear! Mercy sakes! I'm sorry!" Castigio fumbled about. "Are you all right?"

"I will be when you get your feet off of my back!" she fussed.

"Oh!" Castigio said and stepped off. Soot got up brushing herself off. "Never mind. We've got to try again. It's the only way out isn't it?"

"I'm afraid so," Castigio said nodding his head.

"Then help him, Prince!" Soot said in a bossy voice and stood back. The surprised cub obeyed. Putting his hands together he formed a step for Castigio's foot and heaved him up as high as he could. Castigio managed to grab hold of a rock that was stuck fast in the side of the hole and swung himself on through into another tunnel!

A burst of light hit his face and a warm blast of air. "Glory be! We've made it to the other side!" he yelled back.

"We're coming!" called the other two, working to help each other into the tunnel.

Castigio looked around and saw that the light was bright and orange. It was shining in from a crevice only a few feet above his head. Stretching up his arm he caught hold of a root that hung down from the ceiling. Feeling with his feet he found several ledges of stone to climb on. And soon he was able to hoist himself up through the opening.

Prince Zip and Soot pushed through the tunnel just in time to see Castigio's feet disappear from sight. They wondered what he would find on the other side!

8

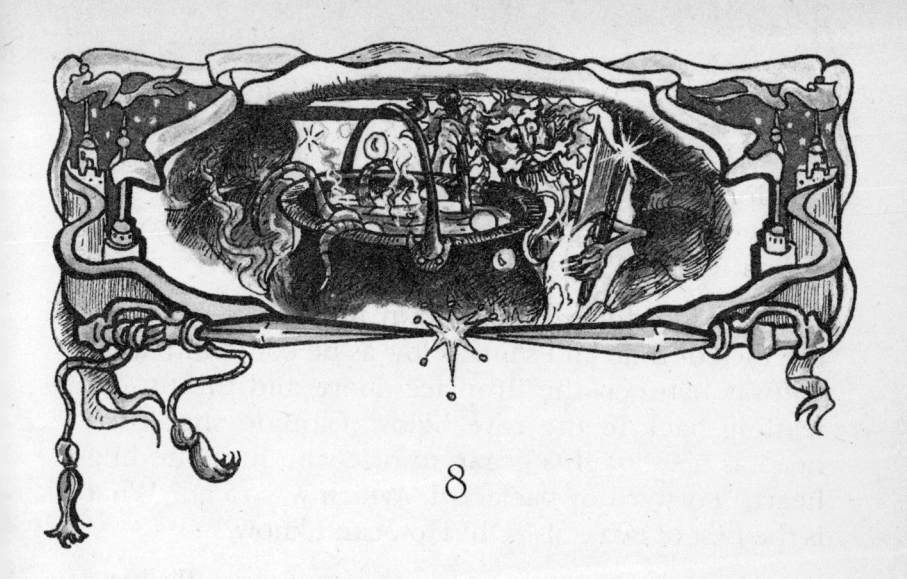

# Pilgrim Soup

The first thing to pop through the opening in the tunnel ceiling was Castigio's helmet. But the second it did, someone snatched it off his head. "Hey!" he yelled and poked his head up to see what had taken it.

"Turtle soup!" wheezed an ancient sounding voice in delight.

Castigio blinked as a scraggly face with beady crinkly eyes stared down at him. It belonged to an ancient little man with a dirty white beard who sat before him tossing Castigio's precious helmet about in his hands. (Castigio had presented his head right through a hole in a huge fireplace hearth!)

"So handy of you to pop in through my hearth, Turtle. Saves me all the bother of catching you!" he cackled and swung a butcher's cleaver wildly through the air toward Castigio's neck.

Castigio ducked back down through the hole in the nick of time and sank as low as he could into a pit halfway between the fireplace above and the tunnel leading back to the cave below. Castigio shook his head as his thoughts began to race with his pounding heart, "Forward or backward? Which way to go? What is the best of two evils? Oh! How can I know?"

He looked up again to see the cleaver flashing about, in search of him, no doubt!

"Certainly Blue Cheetah didn't mean for things to turn out like this!" he murmured, rubbing his adam's apple as it quivered in his skinny neck.

About that time he heard Soot panting too as she struggled to climb out of the dark passageway below. "Castigio, are you up there, friend? Give me a hand will you?" she pleaded. Castigio helped her squeeze through the tunnel and reached back down for Prince Zip. Before he had a chance to warn her, the lamb was on her way up toward the bright orange light.

"Lamb stew!" shrieked the greedy cook in delight again as he saw Soot's fluffy white fleece come into his view. "The pot's already brewing!" added the little man as he reached over the fireplace and gave a bubbling black crock a good swing. Some of the putrid liquid splashed out toward Soot. It would have scalded her hide, if she had not dashed back through the hole in time.

Castigio had not even missed her yet.

Pilgrim Soup

"Turn back!" he was telling Prince Zip, as the poor little cub struggled to climb up from the tunnel.

"What's the matter with you? Are you crazy?" he cried out. "Let me through! I'm exhausted!" Prince Zip managed to get around him and fell at Castigio's feet out of breath.

"Oh, don't go up there, Your Majesty! Your Royal Highness, Prince Zip! It's the most awful sight!"

"What is?" asked the cub trying to understand him.

"There's a crazy man up there with a butcher's knife. He tried to take off my head. He's captured my helmet! He thinks I'm a turtle!" said the flustered Spaniard babbling three times as fast as anyone could understand.

"And he's going to make a lamb stew out of me! The vulgar thing! To think of it! Yikes!" squealed the lamb.

"Oh, Soot, you didn't go up there? I was going to warn you!" exclaimed Castigio.

"I certainly wish you had!" the lamb shrieked.

"I can't tell what you two are quibbling about," Prince Zip said as he stood up. "I will just have to see for myself no doubt!"

"No! Don't!" yelled Castigio and Soot after the adventuresome cub, but it was too late! As fast as lightning, with a single leap, he popped up through the opening so quickly that he even startled the little man, who sat there dipping a string of rat's tails into his crock.

"What a lot of varmints there are in this hearth today!" he wheezed. "Have you come to stay or to go?"

"Depends. To stay I suppose!" answered the cocky cub.

"Well, what sort of soup shall I count on? Do you prefer turtle or lamb or some other? I've had to change my mind a dozen times it seems," said the teetery old man as he leaned forward and emptied out a cupful of rat tails down the hole behind the lion cub's feet.

"What a waste. Tisk! Tisk! They were spoiled and would ruin the broth!" explained the cook. Prince Zip agreed because he liked to eat mice and rats himself.

"Why do you throw them down there?" Prince Zip asked him.

"It's a tidy place to dispose of garbage. I found the hole several years ago when a stone from my hearth loosened up and fell through. Never been down there myself. Is it nice?" cackled the strange little man curiously.

"No, not really!" answered Prince Zip.

"That's as I thought all along. Lucky thing I didn't waste any time inspecting it. It's been rather useful, you know. Lots of critters crawl through the cracks in this fireplace and sometimes I catch a nice-sized one."

Prince Zip eyed him suspiciously, wondering whether or not he had designs on him.

"Now I might have caught you for instance, if you hadn't taken me by surprise. But I would have had to throw you back, because you're too big and probably all fat!"

Prince Zip was glad after all that he had eaten so well in Blue Cheetah's palace. He marveled at the way situations turn out for the best most times.

The cook went on talking as he sliced up some roots and more rat tails. "Things can get messy cutting off heads you know. This hole is rather handy indeed. It saves the mess. I have a recipe for using it. Heads down the hole! Tails in the soup! And I cook the rest!" he explained and went on singing to himself, "Oh, it's heads in the hole! Tails in the soup! Heads in the hole! Tails in the soup! Heads in the...."

"Whose heads?" asked the lion cub thinking of his two friends who were waiting for him down there.

"Why, any varmint who comes for dinner!" wheezed the ancient sprite of a man cackling to himself. It was plain to see that he was insane.

Meanwhile, Castigio and Soot were waiting anxiously in the pit below wondering what had become of their companion.

"Can you hear anything up there?" Soot asked as she watched Castigio climb up halfway to listen.

"Not a thing, Lambkin," he said as he stretched out his toe to balance on a tiny ledge of rock.

"You don't suppose the b-b-butcher...," stuttered Soot, afraid of her own thought.

"No! Mercy sakes! Soot, don't even think it!" said Castigio quickly, for he was thinking the same thing too. "I'll climb up as close as I dare and perhaps I shall hear him alive." He lifted up a foot and meant to reach another ledge when his hand slipped. Losing his balance he fell to the bottom again and landed in a pile of roots and white sticks.

"Oh! Oh! Castigio, are you all right?" Soot hurried to help him up.

"Yes. These old bones of mine have seen worse times I suppose," he said flipping the white sticks away as he climbed out of the pile.

"So have these!" said Soot as she poked her nose about to inspect the pile in which he had landed.

"Bones!" Castigio gasped as he looked over her shoulder. "Skeletons!"

"What kind?" asked Soot trembling in fright. "Are there any of lambs?" she asked timidly.

"I don't want to know, Soot. Mostly it looks like just rats and a snake or two," said Castigio trying to sound as comforting as possible, but he could not hide his trembling hands and shaking knees.

"I don't like this spooky place, Castigio. It gives me the willy-nillies. Why did Blue Cheetah send us here?" said Soot.

Just then a shower of spoiled rat tails fell down upon them as the cook emptied them down the hole.

"O-ou-ou-ou! Ugh!" shivered the lamb as she shook them off of her puffy white fleece. "There's a raving maniac up there who will surely murder us all. We'll never get out alive!" she wailed. Castigio was thinking.

"Shh! Soot, he'll hear you!" said Castigio putting his finger to his lips. "Besides I've been thinking about what the Blue Cheetah said. She said when we got to the other end of the tunnel we'd meet the pilgrim."

## Pilgrim Soup

"Certainly that isn't he! No, Castigio, you don't suppose she meant him?" said Soot doubtfully. "Oh, heaven's sake, my hoofs and curls, I hope not! Not that nasty thing!" she squealed.

"Perhaps so, Soot. We're at the end of the tunnel, are we not? Blue Cheetah has been right about everything else," said Castigio thoughtfully.

"Yes, but we didn't come to the end of the tunnel. That mole caved it in on us, and we came up this other way," she bleated.

"She said nothing was certain, didn't she? Besides we must have been only a few feet from the end of that tunnel as this one was so close to the surface," Castigio paused as he thought some more. "I'm afraid, my dear Soot, that we only missed his front door by a few yards and have come to call on him through the fireplace instead." Castigio didn't like that prospect any better than Soot, but unfortunately he was right, and Soot realized that she had to agree with the logic of it.

"Then what shall we do?" she bleated.

"First of all, we must rescue Prince Zip and then get back my helmet!" said Castigio. He was amazed at how bravely he had said it, but continued on. "I can't really think right without the blasted thing!"

"The lion cub?" asked Soot confused.

"No! The helmet!" said Castigio sorrowfully as he knew he would miss the impish echo.

"How are we going to do it?" said Soot.

"There's only one way. We have to go back up through that hole." Castigio then began to whisper a plan in Soot's ear lest the Pilgrim should overhear them.

137

Up above, Prince Zip was wondering how he might get around to bringing them out of that hole. He was not certain whether the strings of rat tails going into the bubbling crock meant the simpleminded cook had changed his mind about having turtle soup and lamb stew or not. The cub was worried that Castigio and Soot might pop up again at the wrong time and end up in the soup after all. So he kept his mouth shut and listened to the wiry little man babble about the difference between field mice and muskrat tails. It was a subject that interested him slightly anyway as he had once caught them all in the forest.

Prince Zip had crawled away from the hearth by this time and was seated on a well-worn rug beside it. He was watching the cook intently not risking to miss one move. When the crazy little man had finished adding various assortments of tails to the broth, he slapped his knee and got up to reach for a jar on a wooden shelf behind him.

As he did, he teeter-tottered from one leg, swaying dangerously to the other as if he would lose his balance in the end, but did not. Instead he wobbled like a drunkard to the shelf and put forth a long spindly hand with fingernails as long as an eagle's claws. Running his hand across the labels, he knocked a row of jars this way and that until at last he plucked out the jar he wanted and returned to the hearth leaving the shelf in disorder.

"Snails and lice! The spice is right!" he cackled. Unscrewing the lid he pinched a bit of lice and brought it to his lips sucking on it first in a delicious kiss. "Choice! Choice! Choice!" he sighed with pleasure. Then putting in a fingernail, he pierced a snail and sucked it up as well. It must not have agreed with him, however, for he was just as quick to spit it out down the hole. And as he did, he came face to face with Castigio and Soot who were trying to sneak up behind him all that while.

"Ah, ha!" he shrieked. "The turtle's back! The cleaver, cub, the cleaver! Fetch me, the cleaver!" he yelled the snappy order at Prince Zip.

The lion cub was sure to grab it in a flash, but held it out of reach safely as Castigio yanked on the little man's beard and pulled him toward the hole. Soot jumped out and trotted around behind him where she bit his heels and ripped up his britches.

"They've come to take me away today! I knew they would! I knew they would!" he shrieked, "Just let me go. I'll come peacefully. I will. I will!" cackled the little man insanely as he struggled to get free. Then he began to laugh in shrill blasts of laughter. Castigio could not stand the piercing sound. He grabbed his ears with both hands to muffle the laughter, carelessly letting the captive go.

No sooner was the little man free than he jumped for the cleaver. Prince Zip was still on his guard, though, and he held the cleaver high out of reach. Again the little man lunged for it and caught the handle with both hands. There he dangled several inches off the ground swinging with all his might as he tried to use it.

"Clear the way, varmint. I'll git you! You wait and see. Playing tricks on me!" he shrieked.

"No, you won't!" shouted Prince Zip, and with his hind paw he gave him a good whack that caused him to lose his grip and land across the room. When that was safely accomplished Prince Zip threw the cleaver down the hole and hurried to help Castigio to his feet.

"Is it safe to come out now?" Castigio asked as he climbed the rest of the way out of the fireplace being careful not to step on any hot coals.

"Yes, I believe so," Prince Zip assured him. "Without his cleaver he's quite harmless, I think. Loony perhaps but quite harmless."

"What are you doing in my fireplace, varmint?" screeched the little man from the far side of the room as he teetered forward. "I thought you were a turtle!"

"I know you did!" replied Castigio. "And you tried to kill me too! Where's my helmet?" he demanded.

"I haven't seen it!" he snapped and wobbled quickly over to the crock where he stood eyeing them all as if he had something valuable to hide.

"You threw it in there! Didn't you?" Castigio exclaimed.

"There's nothing but turtles in here!" wheezed the wiry little man balancing on one foot while he wrapped the other around it. "Get back, or I'll scratch your eyes out!" he threatened showing his long yellowed nails.

"Mercy sakes! He thinks my helmet is a turtle!" exclaimed the flustered Spaniard.

"It's not a turtle! Give it back to him, you nasty thing!" yelled Soot coming to Castigio's defense. The little man lunged at her and just missed scratching her nose as she ducked behind the lion cub with haste.

# Pilgrim Soup

"Now stand back all of you, or I'll put you in my Pilgrim Soup!" he sneered. Then he clutched his dirty white beard and cackled with delight.

"Is that what you call it?" asked Prince Zip, who had been watching the preparations all the time he had been waiting for the other two. His only answer was cackles and shrieks.

"So that *is* who you are! Castigio was right!" exclaimed Soot.

"You're the Pilgrim, aren't you?" asked Castigio solemnly, for he was greatly disappointed, as they all expected to find a more reverent man.

"You will never be able to help us in that state!" sobbed the lamb as she was now forlorn too.

"You don't...you can't mean...it's not possible that Blue Cheetah sent us all this way to meet this lunatic," stuttered Prince Zip in disbelief.

Suddenly the Pilgrim stopped acting crazy and straightened up rigid. "Who did you say sent you?" he asked for he had heard them after all.

"Blue Cheetah. She lives below. She said we'd find you at the end of the secret tunnel, and we have! Only you are not at all what we expected," said Castigio glumly.

"Not what I expected either," said the Pilgrim.

"Then why do you act this way?" asked Castigio.

"It's a long story, Turtle, but that's not the point. Does she know how I am?" asked the Pilgrim cautiously, as if somehow the thought that she might had brought remorse.

"Well, I really can't say for sure, but she does know where you live and she sent us to get something from you...," Castigio answered.

"I don't know where it is!" snapped the Pilgrim selfishly.

"But you don't even know what we are going to ask you for, do you?" Castigio said, wondering if the Pilgrim could know thoughts like the cheetah.

"Maybe...What else did she say?" asked the Pilgrim with great curiosity.

"She said that you had once traveled most of the way to the Kingdom of the Bright Morning Star and back, and that you could show us the way because that's where we're going!" Prince Zip piped up.

"Then I'd suggest you go right back down that tunnel where you came from unless you want to end up like me!" snapped the Pilgrim and shut his lips tight as if he had nothing more to say.

"So you have been there!" coaxed Castigio as he watched the Pilgrim go back to the fireside to tend his pot.

"You can't leave us wondering like this!" Soot insisted as she saw him reach over the hole and swing a long iron crane across it

Swinging from a hook on the end of the crane, a crock splashed puddles of the stinking broth across the hearth. Smooth stones laid within sizzled and hissed until the putrid liquid had vaporized. Carelessly, the Pilgrim continued to knock the pot about as he stirred it with a ladle.

Sipping the frothy brew he said, "Needs something – not quite right." Then he spied a small snake slithering into a crevice and began to search around for something to catch it with. "Tisk! Tisk!" he sighed at last as he bent over with his hands upon both knees peering into the pit, "Did you have to lose my cleaver? I shall surely starve!"

Prince Zip felt a bit sorry for him, but was grateful to see it go down the hole as he had meant to keep them all alive. "You'll manage somehow," he said indifferently.

"Aren't you going to tell us how to get to the Kingdom?" asked Soot impatiently. She hated to be ignored.

"Anyone for Pilgrim Soup?" asked the jittery old man, changing the subject. Soot could not tell if he had heard her or not.

"Not I," said Castigio weakly, for the odor made him ill.

"Nor, me!" said the lamb.

"Perhaps I'll give it a try," said Prince Zip adding to Castigio, "Someone has to humor him!" Actually, the lion cub was interested in tasting the curious concoction because of all the delicious rodents he had seen the Pilgrim throw in.

Having someone to share his cooking seemed to delight the Pilgrim and he quickly set to putting on the meal. Castigio and Soot watched as he loaded Prince Zip up with a pile of cracked plates from his cupboard. Then he wobbled around stopping here and there as if trying to recall where he had misplaced

"Ah, ha!" the Pilgrim wheezed. "My spoon!"

something. Standing on one foot, teetering back and forth, he would tap his head thoughtfully, then wander about the room searching.

Castigio could now see that the room was actually all there was to a small cottage that stood in bad disrepair. Furniture was strewn like an obstacle course across the floor, and cobwebs hung from the rafters. The Pilgrim was busy turning over tables and chairs until at last he seemed to find what he was searching for. "Ah, ha!" he wheezed. "My spoon! I have only one so you will have to use your tongue!" he told Prince Zip who didn't really seem to care.

The Pilgrim dished out two full bowls of soup and carried them to the center of the room. Rat tails sloshed over the sides as he wobbled along. Soot backed out of his way squeamishly. At last he set the bowls down on the edge of an overturned table and balanced them there while preparing to dine. He motioned for his guest to join him while he teetered on one foot. Losing his balance, he crashed into a pile of pots and dirty pans.

"Mercy sakes! Are you all right?" exclaimed Castigio.

"No bother, Turtle! Happens all the time!" he cackled. "That's why I leave the furniture this way. What's the use of straightening it up once it's spilled each day?" His logic was as clear as cracked glass to the three, but none of them felt as though they wanted to challenge him further.

Castigio and Soot stared at him rudely as he began to enjoy his dinner. Prince Zip took one sip and politely excused himself. The Pilgrim seemed content to be satisfying his hunger and looked up at them from the corner of a beady eye.

"Well, if you won't join me, then have a seat at least, and we shall have our conversation."

"You mean you will tell us what we came to know?" Castigio asked as they all settled upon the dirt floor.

"Maybe," said the Pilgrim and continued on with a tale. "A long time ago, I was interested in these things myself, you see? I was a fruit gardener in this cottage. One day, as I was hoeing the potatoes and rhubarb, a strange reflection caught my eye from the end of the hoe. I looked up to discover a brilliant Star shining in the day.

"My wife was cooking here in this kitchen, and I ran in to let her know. She looked out the window with me, but said there was nothing to see. And yet I saw it plain as day!

"That night and for many nights after, I could see that Star shining like that in my dreams. Beneath it was an incredible kingdom where farmers such as me were selling their harvests. A grand festival was taking place. I knew that I must go there. I told my wife about it every day, but she would not believe me. No, not she! It was her opinion that I was losing my mind.

"One morning when I awoke, she was gone! Poor dear, I can't blame her either, for I was consumed with thoughts of that marvelous thing, and I had frightened her away." Sniffling a little, the Pilgrim paused.

"You must miss her very much," commented Castigio as he looked around the room.

"Sometimes," said the Pilgrim solemnly.

Now Castigio understood why it was in such disrepair and how no housekeeper had kept it.

"Anyway," the Pilgrim continued, "I set out to find the Star that very day. What else was there to do? In my dreams I had seen a passageway through the mountains very near my garden. But when I ran to the spot, it seemed rocky and treacherous. I thought it better to search for another way.

"At last I found a trail that cut through by way of a river and I hiked along its banks. Each day I saw that Morning Star when I awoke, but it was not as close to me as the first time I had gazed upon it. Somehow I felt that it was displeased with the route I had taken. At night when I camped, I had dreams of turning back and taking the trail I had first found, but it seemed ridiculous to double back so I kept going." Prince Zip nodded his head in agreement.

"One afternoon I came to a place where the river emptied into a cave that seemed to cut directly through the mountains," the Pilgrim said. "Just as I was deciding whether or not to explore it, an evil wolf pounced on my shoulders and sent me fleeing into the cave. The deeper I ran the colder it got until at last the river turned to ice, and I found myself slipping down a long way into the cave."

"We've been there!" said Soot excitedly.

Ignoring this interruption, the Pilgrim sipped down another slimy spoonful of the soup. "It is not certain how long I lay there at the bottom. But I had escaped the wolf, and guarding over me was the largest blue cheetah that I had ever seen."

"Tell me, are they usually blue?" asked Castigio curiously.

"On this island they are," answered the Pilgrim. "She had saved my life. But I was still very sore from my injuries. So I stayed there many days. When at last I could walk, it was not very well, for one of my legs had been mangled, and I was terribly off balance. That was when she gave me the sword."

Castigio realized it must be the weapon she had told him about.

"Blue Cheetah gave it to me. It was so marvelous to behold," the Pilgrim continued. "It was forged in the most purest gold and worth a great price I suspect. Carved on its sheathe was a symbol of the Morning Star and a shepherd tending a flock beneath its light. There were many great beasts upon its handle. I was so proud to carry it. It came in handy too as a walking stick to balance me out. Blue Cheetah said I could use it that way, but not to depend on it too heavily as I would need it in battle. She was right.

"Once I found my way out of the cave, I came to a village where there were many sheepherders. I told them I was searching for the Kingdom of the Bright Morning Star. They said that they had heard there was a harvest festival there and thought that it would be a wonderful place to divide their flocks for gain. They decided to accompany me.

"We set out for the highest peak of the mountains to the north and traveled many days. One night we saw the Bright Morning Star. All of us! It was shining brightly over the peak. Just as we were about to take a look over the edge, the great black wolf with a pack of others attacked us out of nowhere. It was the same wolf I had encountered at the river! There he stood, his shadow looming over us in the moonlight. My blood ran ice cold as I stared at his sleek black coat and monstrous jaws! There was a foul stench about him. And the worst were his eyes! Oh, those eyes! Blood red, glowing like the fires of hell!"

Soot shivered, "Abaddon!" she breathed.

"Yes, that is what the shepherds called him. I tried to fight the wolves away, and every one that my sheathe touched lay dead. I never even had to use the blade. The sword had a powerful effect. It was not enough, though, because I could not get to all the devilish beasts in time. They carried away the largest portion of the flock. The shepherds all fled back to the village. I was left alone."

"Where was the wolf?" asked Castigio.

"I thought he had gone off on the chase with the others. At that moment I felt afraid, but then decided I was safe enough. So I climbed over the peak myself and had a look.

"There it was, the Kingdom of my dreams, a dazzling jewel in the middle of a wasteland! The Festival of Harvest was in full swing! The music made me want to sing and yodel at the top of my lungs.

"I began to praise the Morning Star for letting me see its glory. Just as I did, and turned to look for a way into the kingdom, I came face to face with the huge wolf! His snarl struck such fear in my heart that I could not determine which way to go to reach the Kingdom. I began to run. It was no use. He was faster than I was. I had to fight him – there was no way out.

When I turned to face my doom, he was upon me with one pounce. But as we rolled on the ground, I managed to pull out my sword and pierce his shoulder with the blade! He fled yelping in pain. To this day I bet he would remember it!"

"Did you go back to the Kingdom?" asked Prince Zip.

"No," said the Pilgrim, hanging his head in shame. "After my battle with Abaddon, I could not find the way again. We had tumbled a great distance. I was in a deep valley unfamiliar to me. It took me years to find a way out. I survived on rats and bugs that I could kill with my sword."

"What a waste of a weapon!" remarked Castigio who was ashamed for him too.

"Tisk, tisk. So indeed it was," agreed the Pilgrim. "At last I found my way back home and locked myself up tight within, for I was afraid that one day the wolf would come back to finish me off for the wound I gave him."

"And it made you crazy!" said Prince Zip.

"Maybe? You think so?" shrieked the Pilgrim, "Crazy, but not dead!"

"Well, where is the sword?" asked Castigio with interest since Blue Cheetah had said he was to have it.

"I couldn't tell you, Turtle!" snapped the Pilgrim.

"The vines of my garden have grown right through the windows over these many long years and covered everything. It was hidden in them ages ago, because I did not want the wolf to find it here if he found me. I have changed much in my old age and hoped he wouldn't recognize me."

Pilgrim Soup

"Well, you have to find it!" insisted Castigio, "Because Blue Cheetah said I was to have it now and...I must! She said you would give it to me!"

"Why should I?" wheezed the Pilgrim.

"Because we'll take you with us, and you'll have another chance to see the Kingdom," Soot offered.

Castigio could see that the Pilgrim was not going to budge. "What to do? What to do?" Castigio stumbled to his feet to pace across the room. The Pilgrim's beady eyes followed him intently. Looking down, Castigio spied the hole again and whispered, "Blue Cheetah, why did you send us here?"

Overhearing Castigio, the Pilgrim pictured Blue Cheetah to be the next emerging from the hole. Regret filled his heart. What if she found him in this miserable state?

Just then they heard a rumbling coming from the hole. The Pilgrim and Castigio looked on in amazement as the floor of the fireplace hearth began to give way and crumble into the tunnel below.

Jumping to his feet the Pilgrim began to yell, "I'll give him the sword! I will! I will!"

Gratefully Castigio yelled back, "Thank you, Blue Cheetah!"

"Blue who?" asked a voice from the hole.

To their surprise up popped the mole!

"It's you again!" Castigio exclaimed.

"And good day to you too!" replied the mole. "Wrong turn!" he said to himself as he disappeared into the rubble below.

151

The Pilgrim was relieved, but then slapped his hands across his mouth and muttered, "Oh, what have I done?"

"You said you would give us the sword. That's what you've done!" Soot and Zip chimed in together from across the room.

The Pilgrim moaned. Castigio was overjoyed, for now the search could begin for the precious weapon. But glancing down he recalled another matter as well.

"Would you happen to have an extra pair of stockings and bloomers anywhere? Perhaps you could find some while you're looking for the sword."

"Help yourself, Turtle!" said the Pilgrim in defeat. "If you can find them, they're yours."

Then he wobbled across the floor to begin the search. They all began to clear away vines with their hands. Castigio found an oak chest beneath a window covered with ivy. Opening the lid, he was pleased to find a pair of bloomers, stockings and a rusty gray helmet about the size of his own. He whisked them out of the chest and pulled them on with haste. To his pleasure they were a perfect fit.

"They even sag in all the right places like mine!" he exclaimed.

"Where did you get that helmet?" barked the little man selfishly. "You can keep everything else, but you'd be a regular thief to take that!"

"You have kept his somewhere!" said Soot defensively. "So it seems a fitting exchange to keep yours!"

"Oh, bother!" grumbled the Pilgrim and let it go at that.

Just then, as they searched for the sword, a magical miraculous thing began to happen. The garden's vines started shrinking back through the windows and the little Pilgrim's garden became fruitful again. Stunned and amazed, his heart began to soften. A tear rolled down his cheek as he recalled the beauty and joy of his garden so long ago forgotten. It was there that he first encountered the Star and dreamed of finding its Kingdom.

Castigio whispered, "It's just like Blue Cheetah said, when you ask for things, believing in your heart they change!"

"Asking for this weapon is no ordinary request," cautioned the Pilgrim. "You are looking for something most powerful that belongs to those that serve the Morning Star. Be careful with it when you find it, if you do. One must practice much to know how to carry it and aim it well. Once your enemies find out that you possess it, they will constantly test your right to keep it."

As he spoke, Castigio spotted a golden object appearing in the corner of the room, as a trumpet vine curled away and receded out the window. He was about to pick it up when suddenly there was a great scratching at the window, then a prancing on the roof and a rumbling down the chimney.

They all froze to listen!

"Run!" screamed the Pilgrim. In that instant Abaddon crashed down the chimney and was upon the little man. Rolling on the floor he screamed, "It's the wolf! He's followed you here and has seen the sword! Take it and flee! Don't worry about me!"

"Run!" screamed the Pilgrim.

Guilt overwhelmed Castigio for leaving the Pilgrim, but he did not know what else to do. If he tried to kill the wolf with the sword, he might stab the Pilgrim instead! So he obeyed the Pilgrim. Grabbing up the glimmering sheathe, he dashed out the door. Prince Zip and Soot followed running as fast as they could.

Behind them they could hear the two wrestling in the cottage, knocking into pots and pans. The three wondered if they would ever see either of them again.

"Maybe we shouldn't have left him!" said Prince Zip.

"Perhaps the wolf will end up in his soup!" said Castigio hoping for the best.

9

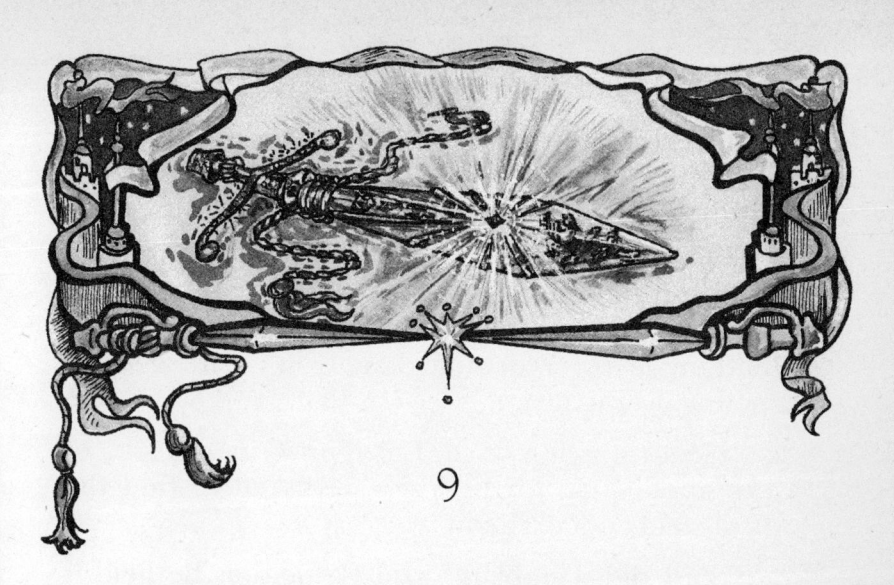

# The Power of the Sword

After the three heroes had fled the cottage and were safely out of earshot, they stopped to catch a breath.

"What a terrifying sight!" Soot exclaimed.

"The wolf?" asked Castigio.

"Or the Pilgrim?" asked Prince Zip, huffing and puffing for they had run till he was out of breath.

"Oh, the both of them!" Soot said. "For a moment there I thought they would finish their quarrel, and then the winner would have a feast of us all!"

"I don't know which would have been worse – to be eaten by Abaddon or to end up as Turtle Soup!"

remarked Castigio as he fiddled with his new stockings and rubbed his neck uneasily.

"Neither one!" said Prince Zip. "The point now is to be seen, my friends! We escaped by the magic of your sword Castigio. Now we must find our way to the Kingdom of the Morning Star. Don't you see? It's watching over us again!"

"He's right for once, Castigio! Our way out of there opened up for us when we asked to find the sword!" said Soot excitedly.

"So it did, Lambkin!" said Castigio as he held it up proudly for all to see.

"Let's have a look at it!" said the curious lion cub as he grabbed selfishly for it.

"Not so fast, my friend," Castigio reminded him. "I found it, and Blue Cheetah gave it to me!"

"So she did!" said the jealous cub. "But do you know how to use it? She said you had to know how to use it!"

"He will learn! He will have to practice!" Soot spoke up defensively. "Let us all have a look at it first!"

Castigio carefully turned the sheathe over in his hand, as the lamb sniffed it and Prince Zip looked on longingly.

"It's fit for a prince, I'd say!" exclaimed the lion cub admiring it.

"Yes, it seems that a prince should have owned this, doesn't it?" Castigio mused. "I wonder how old this is and how Blue Cheetah came by it to begin with?"

# The Power of the Sword

"Look Castigio, there is carving on the handle. It seems to tell a story, or several stories!" observed Soot. "If we could understand, maybe we would understand the power behind the sword and from where it came."

"Seems likely," said Castigio as he turned the sword over again. On the golden handle there was a star encrusted with many small diamonds and jewels. As he studied it more closely, it began to sparkle brighter. Castigio looked up at the sky to see what light the sword reflected. He then realized they were standing beneath the starry spread of night. In their haste to flee the cottage they had not even noticed the time of day.

Castigio searched the horizon excitedly for a glimpse of the Morning Star if by chance he might find it there. He saw nothing but the endless Milky Way of very ordinary stars, all quite beautiful but none so spectacular as the one he sought.

"What are you doing?" Soot inquired as she stared up at him.

"It's night," Castigio answered her as he continued to view the vast distance stretched out before them.

"It is nice enough to know that, but what are you doing?" she asked again.

In disappointment Castigio answered her. "Well, it seemed while I was looking at the star on this sheathe, it sparkled a little brighter than before, and I thought that maybe the Morning Star was here again."

"It must have been your imagination," Soot consoled him.

"Yes, I must remember to be sensible and not let it run away with me," Castigio agreed.

"Look here!" exclaimed Prince Zip. He had been busy studying the sword.

"See here! Look how this golden handle is twisted into a braid at the end and see how the braid of gold is laced with these strips of leather? They make a design like rays of the sun or of a star, don't they?"

"Yes!" breathed Castigio with keen interest as he leaned closer to look at what the lion cub had discovered.

"Well, turn the sheathe over again and see how it is carved. There is a shepherd with a harp. He has sheep at his feet. They are on a hill under the rays of that star!" The cub turned the sheathe back over and traced the rays and the braid of gold back up to the jeweled star on the handle. "And there's more at the bottom...."

In a burst of excitement, Castigio interrupted Prince Zip.

"The hill, Your Royal Highness! The hill! The hill! The hill!" Castigio exclaimed as he did a little jig flapping his hands about wildly with joy. "It's the hill!"

"How do you know that?" said Soot in confusion.

"I feel it in my bones!" Castigio sang out as he picked her up and whirled around in a circle.

"Yes, but how do you kno-o-o-o-w?" insisted the lamb as he spun her about till she was dizzy.

"Well, look! We are on a hilltop here. Are we not?" Castigio reasoned.

Soot and Prince Zip looked around them to find that he was right.

"I have been on this same hill before. I know I have! It was here that I stopped to take in the serenity of this wilderness on my first night on this island." Castigio grew more excited as he began to recognize the familiar spot. He pointed to the silhouette of a mountain range visible in the moonlight. "See! Over there in the distance are the high peaks of the northern mountains just as the Pilgrim said! That is where I hiked the night I first saw the Star!"

"Are you sure?" asked Prince Zip excitedly.

"Yes! and remember that Blue Cheetah said the way out was a long way up? It seemed that we climbed much further up than we slid down into the cave. Her secret tunnel has brought us most of the way! We have come out in the mountains themselves!"

"Oh, thank heavens!" said the weary lamb, "Then we are almost there!"

"See what else is on the sword, Castigio!" begged Prince Zip.

They bent down to examine it again and saw that indeed the hill was much like the one on which they stood and that it was divided down the middle.

"We must be near the pass that the Pilgrim said he first found close by his garden and the cottage!" Castigio observed. "The pass must be the place where the hill is divided here." And he pointed to the picture carved on the sheathe. "It's important that we take this path and not some other as the Pilgrim made the mistake to do." They all nodded.

"I say let's find it tonight. The sky is clear. The moon is shining. We can see clearly enough!" reasoned the lamb.

"But wait, Castigio!" Prince Zip stopped them. "There is more on the sword to decipher! There are four purple rings below the handle and the faces of lions and eagles and...."

Soot interrupted him, "Yes, yes, it's just an extra design to finish the handy work in a pretty fashion. Castigio has already found the message we need in the most important part about this hill. We are just wasting time dawdling here. The sooner we find the pass the safer we'll be from the wolf."

"You are right, Soot," agreed Castigio nervously as he picked up the sword and strapped it to his waist. "We must keep moving. There will be time to look at the rest of the carvings later. Come on let's find the pass."

"Not so fast!" protested Prince Zip. "The purple rings and the lions' faces could have something to do with me and my inheritance! I want to see!" With that, he bounded to Castigio's side and grabbed the magical sword by the handle just as the Spaniard was fastening its buckle.

Before Castigio could stop him, the eager lion cub had pulled the sword halfway out of its sheathe with a great jerk. As he did, a white flash of light burst out from it and knocked Prince Zip backwards, head over tail. Castigio and Soot watched in amazement. The cub rolled end over end down the hill, glowing with a halo of blue. So great was the jolt of lightning from the sword that it had knocked itself free from

## The Power of the Sword

Castigio's buckle as well. Soot pulled Castigio away from the sword by tugging at his bloomers. They stood watching until it stopped glowing.

"Help! Somebody help me!" Prince Zip called.

"Where did you go, Your Majesty?" Castigio answered back.

"I'm down here! Hurry!" Prince Zip yelled. "We're coming!" called the lamb excitedly leaping around to see what had become of him.

"Look over there in those bushes!" said Castigio spotting a ring of evergreens at the bottom of the hill.

Straight through the middle of them was a path of torn and broken branches. Soot and Castigio rushed to the spot to discover a trail blazed through it with pieces of orange fir still clinging to the branches. The burst of power from the sword had sent Prince Zip hurtling like a bullet through the bushes. Prince Zip was not able to stop rolling until he had reached the bottom of the hill. There he lay helplessly caught in a bush, struggling to get free.

"Help me! Don't just stand there! Do something!" he moaned.

Castigio and Soot hurried to free him.

"What happened to you, friend?" Castigio asked.

"It was that weapon! Did you see how it bit me?" Prince Zip cried. "It's more powerful than we thought. Why, who can learn to use such an unpredictable thing? We had better ditch that rascal fast before it kills us all!"

"Ditch it? We dare not!" exclaimed Castigio, "Blue Cheetah gave it to us for a very important battle or

163

The burst of power from the sword sent Prince
Zip hurtling like a bullet through the bushes.

two. She said we must have it to get safely through the mountains!"

"Then who shall carry it?" asked Prince Zip fearfully.

"Castigio, of course!" said Soot, volunteering him again. "Blue Cheetah said he was to use it. He is the worthy one!"

Prince Zip frowned because he considered himself more noble and fit, being a prince. However, he dared not argue, for the sword itself had settled that point, and he did not care to try his paws at it again.

Nevertheless, Castigio was having doubts of his own as well. "Maybe you should carry it after all, Prince Zip. It surely belonged to a prince before or at least a soldier far more noble than I. Go ahead and take it. Won't you?" Castigio did not want to admit now how frightened he was of the sword too.

"Nonsense!" interrupted the lamb. "If you were not worthy, Castigio, then Blue Cheetah would not have given it to you. Surely in the hands of the right master its powers can be controlled. She couldn't have sent us on this mission just to kill us!"

"But did you see it, Soot? It has two edges. They're sharp! And the hand that guides it in battle must be lightning fast to keep from dropping it. My hands are old and feeble. I've never used such a weapon before. Why, it might kill somebody!" Castigio gasped. "Kill...some...body?" he repeated to himself. "Body? O-oo! Mercy sakes!"

"Who?" quipped the cub, backing away. He remembered the duel they'd had on the day they met.

"Of course it's going to kill somebody...Abaddon, the wolf, if we should meet him again. Why do you think she gave it to us, silly?" said the lamb.

"Castigio, you are welcome to have it! It is clear that you are the rightful owner," offered Prince Zip, who no longer wanted the responsibility of carrying the sword. "Perhaps the Morning Star will help you somehow."

That was a comforting thought, and it reminded Castigio of his pledge to Blue Cheetah not to let her down. He decided that for better or worse, he would take charge of the sword again.

"Mercy sakes! Friends, the sword! We left it unguarded on top of the hill!" Castigio suddenly remembered and dashed back up the slope scrambling up on his hands and knees.

To his relief he found the precious sword lying in the moonlight sparkling brightly just where Prince Zip had dropped it. Castigio bent down cautiously and picked it up. Nothing unusual happened. He sighed with the feeling that it was safe to carry it once more. Then he noticed that when the bolt of lightning from the sword had knocked it from his side, it had also melted the buckle. From then on Castigio was forced to carry the weapon in his hand.

"I wonder...," Castigio said looking down at the sword suspiciously. "Did you plan this to happen this way so that I would have to get used to your power in my hands? I wouldn't be surprised," he mumbled to himself as he started back down the hill toward his friends, wondering when he might be called upon to use it.

10

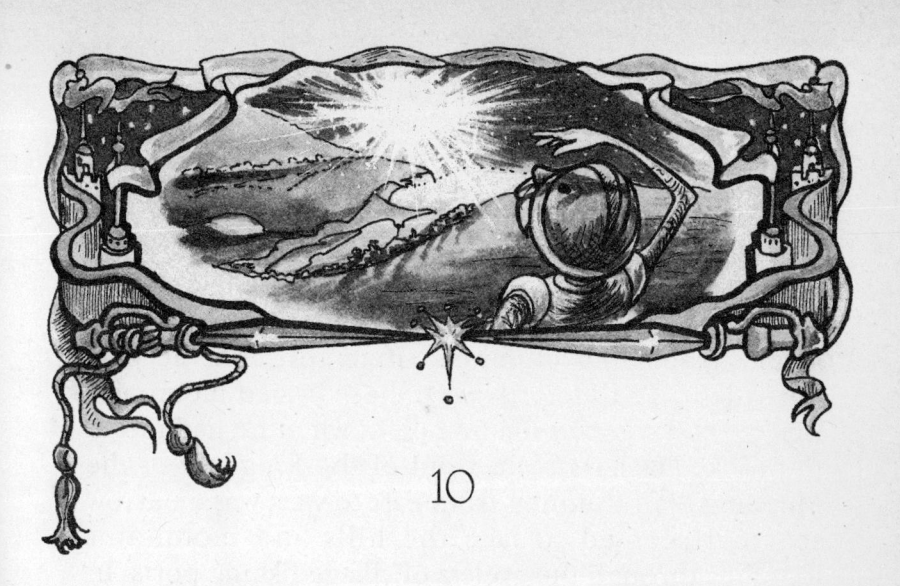

## Discovering the Pass

**C**astigio had expected to find Prince Zip and Soot waiting for him at the bottom of the hill. But they were nowhere in sight!

"Lambkin! Your Majesty?" he called them.

"Soot?...Prince Zip?" But there was no answer. "Oh, do answer me somebody, do! Has Abaddon eaten you alive because I left the sword behind?" Castigio worried aloud, feeling very guilty already in case he should not find them.

When no answer came to him, Castigio turned and ran back up the hill, thinking that perhaps they had gone back there to meet him some other way.

Again he scanned the horizon as he had earlier that night.

It seemed that he could see more clearly now. He was able to make out the faint outline of a few villages to his west. They appeared to be sleeping quietly while smoke from their chimneys sifted through the pale blue night. To the north were those jagged mountains that he had climbed the first night when he had found the rocky glacier scar in front of the Kingdom of the Morning Star. Running from east to west was a narrow sea that seemed to lace the hills and mountains together through the eyelets of village fishing ports. In the east was a dense forest. To the south Castigio could see the roof of the Pilgrim's cottage a long way behind him. Its endless fruit gardens were in full bloom again, seeming to grow for miles right up to the very base of the hill on which he stood. All the countryside around him was in full view in the moonlight. But there was no trace of the lion or the lamb.

"What has happened to you, my friends? Why, you could have gone in any direction. How will I ever find you now? Where should I start looking?" he said in a very lonely voice.

Just then Castigio heard footsteps approaching from the direction of the villages and the sea. With joy he ran to that end of the hill and looked anxiously down the side hoping to greet them. He heard the bleating of a lamb and rejoiced.

Tall grasses growing on the slope hid the lamb from view as he watched to see her head pop through.

"Soot, is that you my friend?" Castigio called.

"For whom are you looking?" came the reply, but it was the voice of a young man. Castigio saw it was a

# Discovering the Pass

shepherd emerging from the tall grass carrying a lamb on his back. Castigio hid the sword behind his back and was glad he had gone back for it before this stranger happened upon it.

"I heard you calling for someone who seemed to be lost, so I came this way to help you," said the gentle man. Castigio stared up at him. He was much taller and had kind eyes and a strong face, one you could admire.

"Are you lost?" asked the Shepherd again.

"Uh, no!" lied Castigio not wanting to appear as foolish as he felt standing up there calling out to the wind. "It's my friends that are lost. I'm finding them."

"So you are," said the Shepherd in a way that made Castigio feel as though his lie had covered up nothing.

"Well, we were all lost together," Castigio said shyly. "But now they are more lost than I. Have you seen them by any chance?"

"Perhaps. I have traveled a great distance searching for someone I lost too, a little white sheep. I've been to all the villages and back looking for her. I just happened to find this one along the way," explained the Shepherd. "If you can tell me what your friends look like, maybe I can tell you if we crossed paths."

"What did the sheep look like that you lost?" asked Castigio curiously, for it began to dawn on him that this might indeed be Soot's Shepherd.

"She is actually a lamb and her flock told me that she was covered with black ashes. She ran away for the shame of it. I do not know what she looks like now, but

"Are you lost?" asked the Shepherd.

# Discovering the Pass

when I see her again I will recognize her," said the Shepherd.

"Well, really, there is only one friend that I have lost," lied Castigio again, for he was very embarrassed about losing Soot too. He had promised to take her to her Shepherd. Now they had met, and the promise was broken for he had lost her.

"I thought I heard you calling for two," said the Shepherd. Castigio knew that he could see through the lie somehow, but because he did not want to seem more foolish by admitting to it, he kept fibbing.

"No! You see my friend just had two names, and when he is lost he comes by either one," Castigio said, not looking at the man's face as he spoke. "He's a very mixed up little creature, just a young thing, a lion cub."

"Well, where do you think you lost him then?" said the Shepherd helpfully.

"Down that path between those bushes," said Castigio pointing to the bushes and broken branches.

"Um...it seems he had a nasty fall," observed the Shepherd. "Perhaps one of the wild beasts around these parts attacked him there."

"What kinds of wild beasts?" asked Castigio nervously.

"Wolves, buzzards, and hyenas!" said the Shepherd. "The worst is a great black wolf. That is why I am searching so long and hard for my little lamb. Are you certain that you have not seen her in your travels, my good man?"

"No!" Castigio lied again. He wanted to say yes. Yet he hated to be caught in a lie, so he determined that he would watch the Shepherd when they parted to see which way he went. Then if he could find Soot, he would be a hero and return her to him as quickly as possible. Everything would work out well in the end he hoped.

"Well, if you happen to see her, please be her friend. She will need a brave one who will defend her from these beasts if indeed it is not already too late," said the Shepherd.

"Oh, mercy sakes!" Castigio gulped at the thought of it. "Uh, if I find this friend of yours, where shall I direct her?" he asked.

"Oh, please do not turn her out on her own! It is too dangerous!" said the Shepherd. "Would you be a good man and see her home for me? I can reward you richly and make the journey worth your while!"

"That's not necessary," said Castigio quickly, because he was feeling very guilty already and didn't feel worthy of a prize. Besides, Soot was his own dear friend, and he had determined to do this for that reason alone. "Just tell me where to meet you if I find her again."

"Again?" asked the Shepherd.

"Oh, I mean again for both of us. You had her once and I will find her for you again," covered up Castigio.

"Well, I certainly would appreciate it, my good man. It is a lot to ask of you," said the Shepherd with reserve.

"Oh, no! No! It isn't!" Castigio assured him, determined now more than ever, to find her and right his wrong. "If you could just tell me where to find you again...."

The Shepherd looked at him a long time as if he were trying to see right through him. Castigio couldn't stand it. He didn't know when he had ever told such a lie before. He was just about to break down and confess for the pain of it, when the Shepherd answered him at last.

"Have you ever heard this said, 'The beams of a morning star are straight and true and so are the words of a wise man too; Shining light on hidden places, speaking well in strangers' faces.'?"

"No." Castigio winced. He fidgeted with embarrassment as he prepared to confess, but was instead surprised by the Shepherd's forgiving generosity.

"Your name *Castigio* means "little castle." The one who named you has called you brave when you as yet were not. But, indeed, you will be a strong fortress and a help to this friend whom you have lost. And when you find her, I think you can be trusted, my good man," he said.

Castigio could not remember telling the Shepherd his name. He marveled at the revelation of its meaning "little castle." To know it made his skinny old chest swell with a new bit of hope. The Shepherd seemed pleased.

"Over there behind that tallest mountain is a secret city that very few know about. It is open for everyone, but it is best that no cowards enter in. It is a place for brave and truthful men," he pointed across the hill to the northern mountains. Castigio took notice, all the while marveling at this man. How was it that he, a simple shepherd dressed in rags, seemed somehow more gracious than anyone he had ever met? With increasing interest Castigio listened.

"I am going there now to take my flocks to the Harvest Festival. I've spent all the time that I can, staying behind to look for this lamb. Now I must hurry to collect the flock from some shepherds who promised to watch them for me. And I have to find out where this little one I found today belongs."

The Shepherd was telling Castigio everything that he had wanted to know.

"The city was built there because of its perfect location to defend its treasures from intruders. The only hardship is that too many men are not brave enough to seek it out and cross the mountains. See here...," the Shepherd set down the lamb. He put his hand on Castigio's shoulder and walked him to the north side of the hill. "Here is a pass. It leads to the sea out there."

Castigio noticed he pointed right to the spot where the lion cub had blazed a trail between the bushes.

"These bushes have grown up here since I passed by last. But it seems that your friend was fortunate enough to fall in the right place and open up the pass again!" said the Shepherd with delight. "Perhaps if you follow his trail you will find him already on his way!"

"Mercy sakes! Yes!" exclaimed Castigio, feeling that providence was with them again. "Then where do we go?" he asked.

# Discovering the Pass

Cross the sea in front of that fishing village over there and follow the main street straight to the foot of the mountain."

"Is there any other way?" asked Castigio curiously, because he thought he had previously reached the Kingdom from that hill before without crossing the sea.

"Yes, there are other roads and passes that would keep you in these hills for days until you made your way around the sea. But this is the most direct route," the Shepherd said.

"How do we cross the mountain?" asked Castigio.

"Walk straight up the face. Then look for the place where the white eagles make their nest," said the Shepherd. "When you pass it, you will be on the right side of the mountains. Watch out for the gray buzzards though, for they nest nearby. You may have to fight them, because they do not like strangers to pass by. Be especially watchful of their talons, because they are full of deadly venom like a hunter's poison spear."

Castigio shivered at the thought. "Tell me, Shepherd, aren't there any nice peaceful places to walk about on this island? Everywhere I have been since we landed seems so hostile, even the towns."

"Was it any better where you came from?" asked the Shepherd.

Castigio thought of the ship and El Capitan and thought, "Certainly not!" Then he thought of Spain, his homeland and was sure there had been some good times at least in the days of childhood. "Well, somewhat better I suppose," he answered.

"The closer you get to the secret city, the harder life may be for you, friend. It is the only true haven of peace of which I know. It is truly worth the battle to reach it, believe me!" said the Shepherd as he stared across the valley longingly.

The Shepherd continued. "The black wolf and his evil pack are very jealous of the city. Before the city was built here, he had free run of this island. But he terrorized everyone who lived here. One day he attacked a gentle shepherd attending his flock of sheep and mauled him to death."

Castigio wanted to know more about the tragedy of the shepherd, but dared not interrupt the sacred tale.

"After that the Morning Star determined that the wolf should never roam the Kingdom unguarded again. The city and fortress were built in a day to protect all who would choose to enter in, and he was forbidden to pass through its gates. Every time he tries, a bright beam of light shoots down upon his path so that he can not find a way to enter in.

"He fears the lions that guard the city and the people that find it, because one day one of them may kill him. He feasts on the lambs that the villagers raise. And he fears he may starve, if they should ever discover the way into the city to safely herd their flocks there," the Shepherd finished.

"How do you know so much about the wolf?" asked Castigio, because everyone he had met until that time had only spoken of him.

"I have fought him myself. Anyone who ever confronts him needs to know as much about him as possible. It is the only way to defeat him!" said the Shepherd solemnly.

Castigio shuttered, "Mercy sakes! I hope I never see him again as long as I live, then!"

"If you cross those mountains you will!" predicted the Shepherd.

Castigio hoped he was wrong, because he had to cross them to fulfill his promise to Soot and Blue Cheetah and Prince Zip and even to make things right with the Shepherd. How had he let himself get so involved? Why couldn't he have just forgotten about the Star anyway?

Castigio was thinking about how sorry he felt for himself when the Shepherd spoke up again and said he must be going.

"If I see your friend I will take him to the secret city with me, and we will meet you there," said the Shepherd as he waved goodby and picked up his lamb.

Castigio waited and watched as he headed down the pass over the hill. Suddenly the Shepherd vanished before his eyes. Castigio rubbed them hard and reasoned, "He must have run over the edge." Then he started after him through the bushes hoping to find the lion and the lamb.

## 11

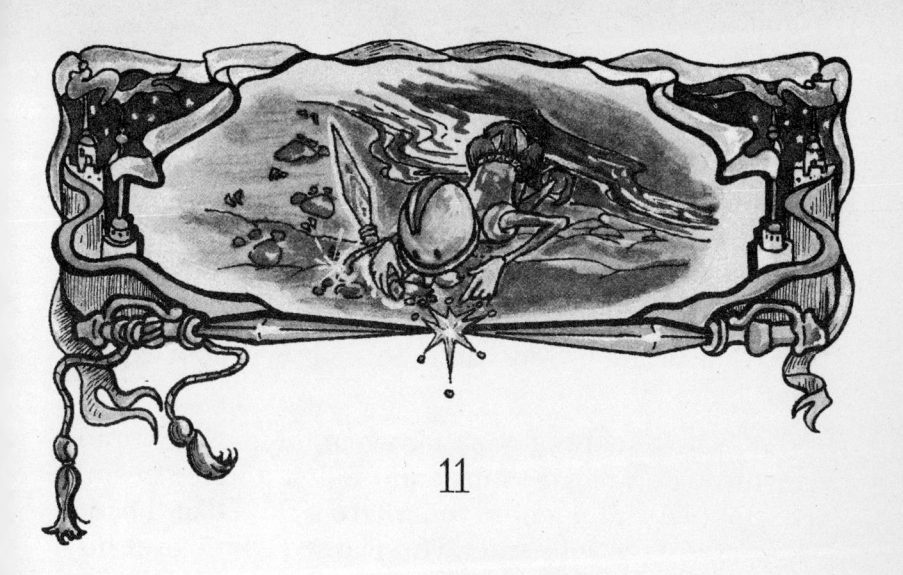

# A Confession

At the bottom of the hill, Castigio looked around once more for Soot and Prince Zip but found no trace.

"What a miserable hero I'd make!" he muttered shaking his head in despair. Kicking at the dirt, he thought of his valiant speech to Soot along the road.

"We were like an egg and a yoke! A tooth and a grin! A smile and a dimple! Friends to the end! Oh, Soot, I'm so sorry. I've lost you. How lonely I am," said Castigio sadly.

"If you could see me now, you would know I was no friend," Castigio sobbed aloud. "I could have at least asked the Shepherd to help me find her. Why didn't I?" he asked himself miserably. "It will serve me right if I should never see her again." He swished away a salty tear as it landed on his mustache. Then he shuffled his feet slowly and began to walk along the pass in the direction the Shepherd had gone.

"Maybe he'll find you!" he said as if Soot could hear him.

Castigio had not gone far when the pass began to cut through a narrow valley and follow a little stream. He stopped a moment to see where it flowed and bent down to sip the cold water. He splashed a little over his face to stay awake. He had begun to feel sleepy.

"Stay awake, old fool!" he said slapping his chin, "You can't fall asleep here. You've got to find them before some beast does." As soon as he had said that he wished he hadn't, for he remembered he was all alone too. Thinking about such things made him nervous again, and he began to notice how alive the bushes were around him with the sounds of crickets chirping and frogs croaking. Castigio felt as if a thousand eyes were watching him.

He stood up and looked about uneasily. The bushes in this part of the pass had begun to look more like a forest to him. And he saw that the stream ahead was overshadowed by a dense umbrella of trees. Their limbs were tightly woven together like spider's webs. The way before him looked very shadowy and dark.

Castigio searched his heart for some courage and found it rather empty. He began to wish he had never heard of conquistadors or the Fountain of Youth, because he did not feel at all like an explorer now. He wished that he was in the bottom of the ship again hiding in his pickle barrel on his way back to Spain. At

# A Confession

least there he knew his way around and was pretty good at avoiding El Capitan. Why had he joined up with that band of sailors anyway? His whole life seemed like such a mistake. Nothing had ever worked out for him.

"What makes you think I can find your old Kingdom anyhow, you Morning Star? Maybe, you're just a figment of my imagination!" he shouted.

Instantly Castigio covered his mouth with both hands, for he had not meant to be so loud. He quickly looked over his shoulder in each direction to be sure no beast had heard him. A bush beside him rustled, and a large rabbit ran out in front of him as the shout had startled it. Castigio never bothered to see what had crossed his path, but took off in a panic, tripping over the creature as it fled. He fell face first into the muddy bank of the stream. Spitting out mud, he wailed in fright, "Oh, Morning Star, where are you now? Have mercy on me, if you can!"

Castigio felt a breeze blow through the dark covering of trees over his head and looked up to see the branches bending back against it. An opening in the leaves revealed the starry sky, and for a moment he thought he could see the glow of the Morning Star. He blinked and decided there was nothing there after all. But suddenly he felt at peace and much safer than before.

Castigio picked himself up and brushed off the mud. His hand was still closed tightly around the sword. He noticed that not a drop of mud had touched it while he was completely covered. "You must exist. Why do I doubt you?" he whispered up at the sky.

One shoe was stuck in the mud, and Castigio bent down again to free it. As he did, he saw a small track beside it much smaller than his own and not large enough to be the rabbit's. It was a hoof print!

"Soot!" Castigio exclaimed. As he studied the print he saw another beside it that was round and padded. "Prince Zip!" Laid out before him was a trail of footprints all the way to the edge of the stream and up the bank on the other side. Castigio yanked the stubborn shoe free and slapped it crookedly on his foot in a hurry. Splashing through the stream, he climbed up the bank as fast as he could manage.

In a clearing at the top was a wonderful sight. A crackling campfire snapped and sputtered happily as it shed its warm light on two sleeping figures nearby. Curled up together in a little ball atop a velvet cape and some blankets were the lion and the lamb.

Castigio could hardly believe his eyes. "Unusual luck!" he murmured softly, looking around to see who had made the fire, and invited his companions to enjoy it. There appeared to be no one else around as he stayed at the edge of the clearing a minute or two watching to be sure he was welcome also. When no one came to tend the fire, he decided they were quite alone and tiptoed over to his friends.

"Soot, wake up!" Castigio tapped her shoulder gently.

"Castigio!" she exclaimed and rolled over a little startled, "I knew you'd come!"

"What are you doing here, Lambkin? I thought some evil beast had snatched you. Why did you run off and leave me all alone back there?" asked Castigio.

A crackling campfire snapped and sputtered happily
beside the lion and the lamb.

Prince Zip was startled by his voice too and awoke with a snarl. "Stand back! Who goes there?" he said leaping on Castigio's back.

"Mercy sakes! It's only me, Your Majesty!" said Castigio slapping the lion cub down with his hand. Prince Zip rolled to the ground in a clumsy somersault.

"So it is! What took you so long?" Prince Zip asked smartly.

"What do you mean, 'What took me so long?' How did you expect me to find you here? I almost didn't!" Castigio scolded.

"Forgive us, Castigio," Soot said, "But we heard this charming music playing right after you went back for your sword. It was so unusual, we forgot everything else. We just had to see from where it came...."

"It was so loud that we were sure you'd hear it easily enough and know that was where we'd gone...," interrupted Prince Zip.

"What music?" asked the bewildered Spaniard.

"I'm getting to that part. Now let me finish," said the lamb. "At the bottom of the hill we began to look around for the pass. We walked just a few steps down this path to see where it would lead while we waited for you. We meant to come back, of course," she assured him, "except just then we heard this wonderful music and thought it might be the Harvest Festival of the Kingdom that the Pilgrim told us about. The music stopped and there was no one around. There was only this cozy fire, a robe and bedding here. Prince Zip said that the music had been so loud that

## A Confession

Prince Zip said that the music had been so loud that you had surely heard it on your way behind us and that we might as well stay and warm up while we waited for you. I was cold, but I looked back to see if you were coming. When my head was turned, that curious cat took off toward the fire as quick as a rat!" Soot stopped to give Prince Zip a displeasing look. "I had to follow him or I would have been all alone in the dark!"

Prince Zip turned his guilty head and covered his embarrassment with a yawn.

"We're sorry, Castigio! We didn't mean to fall asleep. We just couldn't help it," said Soot sincerely.

"Don't you know you could have been bewitched? Maybe there are some witches around this forest with sleeping potion or something! Maybe there's one in the fire and we're breathing its sneaky fumes right this instant!" Castigio warned them. The fire snapped and crackled just then and let out a bright red spark!

"Yikes! Castigio is right!" squealed the lamb and dived back under the blankets to hide.

"Nonsense!" said Prince Zip confidently. "I've lived in forests all my life and never heard of such a thing!"

"Never?" asked the lamb peeping cautiously out from under the blankets.

"Well, I have!" contradicted the Spaniard. "I once saw three of them in a swamp on one of El Capitan's adventures! It was a terrifying sight. You wouldn't want to fool with them!"

"What did they look like?" asked Prince Zip curiously.

"Never mind! I don't want to know!" said Soot ducking under the blanket again.

"And I don't want to tell it!" said Castigio firmly as he did not care to scare himself.

"What makes you think we were bewitched to stop here? Why should we be so full of fear?" asked Prince Zip. "All of us are tired. Aren't we? We deserve to sleep peacefully. Not since we were in the tunnel have I even had a cat nap! And then it was the mole who interrupted that with his mishap!"

"The music you spoke of seems to have lured you here surely enough, but for what purpose? Doesn't it seem mysterious that it stopped when you arrived and that there's no one here? How do you know that the robe and bedding you sleep on does not belong to some ogre, who means to wrap you up in them when you are asleep and roast you in the fire?!" Castigio reasoned.

"Ogre?" bleated the lamb. "Oh, no!" and she pulled the covers tighter around her head until only her fluffy white tail was showing.

"I doubt it!" said Prince Zip folding his paws across his chest. Then he strutted over to the pile of blankets and gave the bundle where Soot was hiding a good kick.

"Ouch!" came the reply from the blankets. Prince Zip picked up the robe and tossed it to Castigio.

"Look! It's not ugly enough to belong to a witch. And it's not big enough to fit an ogre!" said the lion cub brightly. Castigio had to agree and nodded his head.

# A Confession

"Maybe a little ogre?" trembled the lamb.

"Don't be a worry wart, Soot! I'm afraid Prince Zip is quite right. I have been the fool," said Castigio.

"No, you haven't!" answered Soot defensively. "You were just looking out for us all. We should have been more wise," she crawled out from under the blankets and hugged his knees.

"I wonder who this beautiful cape belongs to then?" asked Castigio as he handed the velvet robe back to the lion cub. Prince Zip nestled it against his cheek and said, "It's very soft."

"Perhaps it belongs to a fine lady or a princess," mused Castigio.

"Or maybe a shepherd," added Soot.

"No, he didn't wear one...," said Castigio absent-mindedly.

Soot whirled around, "You mean you saw him? My Shepherd?"

Castigio had not meant to tell her of it at all. He had simply intended to find her and lead her safely back to meet the Shepherd at the Kingdom of the Bright Morning Star.

"When, Castigio? Where?" begged the lamb excitedly. "Is he nearby? Oh, tell me. You saw him back there, didn't you? Oh, where? Where? Where?"

"Soot. Oh, dear little Soot," was all Castigio could say. He hung his head in shame because he felt so guilty and so sad for her.

The lion cub looked up with a puzzled expression. Soot stopped dancing about and stared at the Spaniard too.

187

"Tell me, friend, where?" she gently coaxed him.

"Up on the hill," said Castigio solemnly as he patted her head and took a long breath. "He heard me calling for both of you, when I couldn't find you after you'd run off...."

"Oh, no! It's all my fault. I've run away from him again!" sobbed the lamb.

"Now, now. There, Soot. Please don't cry," said Castigio sympathetically. He went on to tell his tale. "Your dear Shepherd said he's been looking for you, Soot, and he truly has forgiven you. I just couldn't tell him where to find you, because you were lost again."

"Oh, it wasn't your fault, Castigio. It was mine," she cried and buried her face in between her hoofs as she sank down to the ground. Prince Zip brought the robe to wipe her tears for even he was touched.

"Oh, dear. Yes, it was my fault!" confessed the Spaniard. "I didn't even tell him that you might be nearby, because I did promise to watch over you, my friend, and see you safely to him. I was too embarrassed to let him know how I had failed you. Oh, please forgive me, Soot!"

"It doesn't matter now," wept the little lamb helplessly, "I forgive you."

"Well, where did he go, Castigio?" asked Prince Zip eagerly, "Maybe we can still find him?"

"He showed me the pass to the secret city in the Kingdom of the Bright Morning Star," Castigio said and explained to them how to get there. "Then he started on his way again. I thought I was following his trail when I came to the stream. His footprints vanished, but I found your tracks instead. And they led me here!"

"Well, let's find him then!" suggested Prince Zip.

"He's sure to be far off by now," Castigio said. "And I am not certain if he stuck to this pass or went on searching in some other way. It would be best to see if we could find his footprints in the stream bank when it is morning and follow them then. I know the way to the Kingdom now. We can meet him there," Castigio looked down at the lamb. She had curled up beside him and cried herself into a sorrowful sleep.

"Let's wait for her to wake up, Your Majesty. She will do better then," Castigio said softly to Prince Zip. He stroked Soot's fleece. Prince Zip looked on curiously and lay down beside her too. Soon they were all fast asleep.

## 12

## Sweet Dreams

**W**atching from the shadows of the wood was a black creature. Slinking through the trees and weeds, he moved around the clearing silently waiting for a chance to get closer to the three. Abaddon had found them alone again.

This time he had decided to be more cunning in order to separate them. He would have a better chance of catching them one by one. Seeing they were sound asleep, he moved in cautiously toward the campfire to work out his plan.

Just as he was about to set a toe down next to the lion cub, a spark shot out from the fire and singed his tail. He jerked it back quickly and muffled a yelp with his paw. Prince Zip heard him with his keen ears, though, for he was a light sleeper.

"It's Abaddon! It's Aba...Umph!" Prince Zip tried to warn his companions. But the wolf slapped a black paw over his mouth, before he could shout. He didn't keep it there for long, though, because the lion cub bit hard.

"Get back or I'll rip you to shreds!" said the cub in the most ferocious voice he could manage as he gnashed his little white teeth. The wolf only snickered and laughed in a low voice.

"Come, now, you wouldn't bite the hand of a friend. Would you?" he asked slyly.

"A friend?" asked Prince Zip suspiciously.

"Why, yes, my prince," said the wolf quickly, scheming as he spoke.

"How did you know I was a prince?" asked Prince Zip, more interested in what the wolf had to say.

"Anyone can see your noble face resembles that of the family line in the Royal Lion's Guard," whispered Abaddon as he saw his chance to trick him and not wake the others.

"You know about the Royal Lions that guard the Kingdom of the Morning Star?" asked the lion cub.

"Oh, yes, certainly. All of us royal folk know such things," he lied.

"Are you royal?" asked the cub naively. "I just thought you were evil."

"Really? Who said so?" asked the wolf quietly.

"Blue Cheetah said so," answered Prince Zip.

"Well, she lied, my prince!" said Abaddon cunningly.

"She did?" asked Prince Zip in amazement.

"Yes, she surely did. It was a trick to keep you from your destiny. She meant to keep you busy following these ordinary creatures, so that you would not enter the Kingdom in your own royal style," Abaddon said. "Why, the lions at the gate are waiting for you. They will have a special ceremony just for you alone if they recognize you when you arrive. If you look like a pauper with these peasants, then no one will ever know you are different."

"Oh, my!" breathed the cub anxiously.

"Yes, my prince, it was all a plot!" said Abaddon.

"How wicked of them!" said Prince Zip turning to look at the Spaniard and the lamb. "And I trusted them!"

"Yes! Yes! Those things happen to the best of us," said Abaddon as he put a hairy arm around Prince Zip's shoulder and turned the cub's head away. "Now listen. I am a special ambassador from the Kingdom. I have been sent to bring you back to your rightful parents."

"Truthfully?" asked the cub looking up at the red beady eyes. He was still uncertain that the wolf was really a friend. But he was convinced he shouldn't trust the others. So he listened.

"I swear it," said the wolf. "I am going to take you to a village where many exotic creatures such as ourselves are waiting to join you and me. We are going to ride in a gallant parade through the city, so that every peasant can pay us respect on our way to the Kingdom. And you, my prince, will be the star of the show!"

"Me?" asked the tickled cub. He was very flattered and swelled out his little chest with pride. "Am I erratic?"

"Exotic!" corrected Abaddon.

"Exotic?" asked the lion cub again.

"Yes, most certainly!" lied the wolf.

"And they are not?" asked Prince Zip glancing back over his shoulder at Castigio and Soot, who were still sleeping soundly like two little logs.

"They certainly are not, the silly things!" said Abaddon distastefully. "And they have nearly ruined your reputation!" he lied.

"How so?" asked Prince Zip.

"Lions are ferocious and great hunters! Don't you know?" asked the wolf cleverly.

"Why, no. No one ever told me so," said Prince Zip.

"Of course, they didn't. They didn't want you to know it," the wolf assured him. "Lions kill lambs, my dear!"

"Oh, no!" exclaimed Prince Zip in shock. "They...They...do?" he stuttered.

"Yes!" Abaddon said. "And what do you think the royal guard would have thought of you if they'd seen you walking up to the Kingdom gates in the company of that silly lamb? They would have said you were a regular sissy! Alas, no ceremony for you, my friend."

"That would have been terrible!" agreed the foolish lion cub.

"Why, who ever heard of a lion lying down with a lamb?" mocked the wolf.

"Certainly not I!" said Prince Zip proudly not wanting to look foolish.

"Quick, grab your cape. Let's be off before they wake up and try to stop you!" said the wolf eagerly, for he was certain now that he had Prince Zip convinced.

"My cape?" asked Prince Zip dumbly. "Uh, yes...," stuttered the wolf searching for a quick explanation for he had mistakenly thought that the robe on which the cub had been sleeping was his own. "Don't you recognize it?" he asked hopefully.

Prince Zip bent down to examine the velvet robe again. He noticed now that it was purple. "It's purple!" he exclaimed. "Do the Royal Guard wear purple?"

"Oh, yes! Yes, they do!" lied the wolf wiping his brow in relief.

"This was lying here by the fire when we came by. There was no one here to claim it but I," explained the cub.

The wolf saw his chance to take the credit. "I put it there for you, my prince, so that your head would not touch the rocky ground. Only the best is fit for a king!"

"You did?" exclaimed Prince Zip blindly.

"Yes, and I lit the fire too. I waited till you came this way. It was the best plan to rescue you from those others," lied the wolf again.

"That was wonderfully tricky of you," said the lion cub admiringly.

"So it was!" said Abaddon proudly. He could not have been more pleased with how this had turned out. Snickering under his breath, he seized the opportunity to lead the cub away. "Come now, my prince. Soon it will be light. We must hurry to the village, before they catch us!" urged the wolf in his evil cunning voice. Then he slyly turned toward the darker part of the forest. "I know a shortcut. Come!"

Prince Zip snatched up the robe and pranced away with the wolf obediently. At the edge of the clearing, he paused only an instant with a second thought and wondered, *I hope I'm doing the right thing!* Then he thought, *I'll be one of those exotic animals!* and ran off after the wolf.

Castigio and Soot slept on through the night until the song of something as lovely as a bird woke them the next morning. Soot rolled over lazily and twitched her nose at a fly. Castigio thought he was still dreaming the song in his visions of sleep.

"Castigio, wake up!" Soot called him and poked at his bloomers with her hoofs, "Wake up and listen!"

"Uh?" he asked wearily as he stretched his legs and arms.

"Do you hear that music? It's the same that we heard in the path last evening!" she said.

"It is?" asked Castigio excitedly and listened as the beautiful melody drifted through the woods.

"It's coming nearer!" he exclaimed.

"Quick!" said the lamb, "We've got to make ourselves presentable. Straighten up this bedding before the owner sees we've helped ourselves to his fire and things!"

Castigio began to shake out his blanket and tidy up his stockings and bloomers. Then he turned to a frumpled throw beside him and looked for the lion cub to get him ready too.

"Prince Zip! Get up, lazy bones!" Castigio said briskly as he yanked up the cloth. How surprised he was to discover nothing under it but grass!

"Soot, where is Prince Zip?" he exclaimed

She looked around for him too and gasped.

"Lambkin, he's vanished!" said Castigio.

"Let's not get excited!" she said, "Maybe he's taking a bath in the stream!"

"Oh, certainly," nodded the Spaniard as he started down the bank to find him. Then he stopped in his tracks and said, "Lion cats don't like baths! They hate to get wet!"

"Oh, dear!" Where do you think he has gone?" worried the lamb.

"Maybe he set out early to find the Shepherd, Soot. He has a strong mind of his own, that cub!" offered Castigio hopefully. Then added to himself, "Mercy sakes, I hope he is all right!" and thought how he might miss the cocky little cub if he were gone too long.

"Do you suppose?" Soot asked weakly.

"Sure! He's quite the adventurer, you know! We'll see him soon," he said. It was all he could offer her for he had not the slightest notion where they might look for him.

"Then maybe we ought to stay around here until he returns," Soot said thoughtfully.

"Maybe," said Castigio. "But let's hide over there behind those trees until we see what kind of host we shall have if we stay." He hurried out of the clearing with Soot following close behind his heels. She was still thinking of ogres and witches.

They waited quietly for a sign of the musician to appear. By and by the music grew louder. At last they spied a bright red feather moving behind some leaves.

"Maybe it's some kind of bird?" said Soot in a whisper.

"Birds don't build campfires," said Castigio.

Then they saw a flittering gold tassel swish beneath a row of bushes at the edge of the clearing.

It was followed by a pair of milky white legs wearing sandals made of honeysuckle vines. In an instant the purest looking maiden emerged from the woods accompanied by a host of birds and little forest animals romping at her feet. In her hands she held a flute that she sweetly kissed with the breath of her song.

Entering the campfire circle, she stopped playing and seated herself upon a rock. The animals clustered about her feet and paused there too.

"We have visitors this morning," she said in a voice that sounded as if she had almost sung it.

"Wouldn't it be nice if they would stop hiding from us and join our company?" she said looking in the direction of Castigio and Soot.

It was useless to hide. They had been discovered. So they cautiously came out to greet her. Castigio bowed low and graciously removed his helmet. "Pleased to make your acquaintance," he said, trying not to sound nervous. "I am Castigio. This is Soot. And who might you be?"

"Dreams," she said sweetly.

"What about them?" asked Soot.

"What about what?" asked the maiden leaning forward to touch the lamb's fleece.

"Dreams?" asked Castigio.

"Oh," she laughed lightly, "That's my name and my job altogether! I am the guardian of dreams on this island. Haven't you heard of me before?"

Castigio was uncertain and did not know how to answer her. So he shook his head in both directions at once.

"Have a seat by me and I will explain. But first let me finish my business this morning. It must be interrupted no longer," Dreams said. Then she tilted her face to the sky and continued to play silvery tunes for a long time.

Castigio and Soot watched as the birds circled above her head. Many more from the woods joined her. Above them the pinkish clouds of dawn swirled in a breathtaking beauty and began to sparkle as if they had been lined with gold. Wispy clouds of every color of the rainbow sifted up to melt into them. They came out of the lower regions of the sky from the direction of the villages. Then the sky began to spin them together as if it were a weaver's spindle. Faster and faster the clouds spun until the sky above them looked like a marbled sugar frosting!

Castigio gasped in breathless amazement as the whole gathering of clouds vaporized into a mist. And in its place appeared the Bright Morning Star for the briefest instant!

"Did you see it, Soot? The Morning Star!"

"Of course she didn't. It was a dream I gave *you*." Dreams said.

"Where is the Morning Star? I want to see it too!" demanded Soot.

"When you see the Shepherd, Soot, you will find it!" Dreams assured her.

"It was here for an instant behind those clouds. Now it's gone!" said Castigio.

"Well, everything is done for another day," Dreams interrupted them. Putting down her flute she snapped her fingers and a flock of humming birds descended carrying a bouquet of flowers between them. She thanked them and reached out to Castigio and Soot.

"Will you join me for breakfast? The nectar is wonderful," she said.

"What kind is it?" asked Castigio curiously.

"It's heavenly," was all she said.

After sipping a few drops, Castigio and Soot felt as though they had slept a hundred nights instead of one. "I feel so strong!" exclaimed Castigio.

Castigio gasped in breathless amazement.

"You won't need to eat for the rest of your journey. It's the strength of the angels," said Dreams.

"Are you an angel?" asked Soot.

"Would it matter much?" Dreams answered her with a question. Soot didn't know how to answer. So she went back to sipping her nectar until it was all gone.

"Your music, it was so...so...so...." Castigio meant to compliment her, but couldn't find the right words.

"Heavenly?" Dreams responded.

"Yes," Castigio said. "All the music I've heard on this island seems to be that way. It's like listening to a happy brook all the time – so refreshing. I've never heard anything like it before."

"That's the music of the Morning Star," explained the maiden. "He composes it, and the streams and harps and minstrels play it. His music calls everything on this island to guide men toward the Magical Kingdom. Each note is carried on a beam of light that can't be seen, only heard. It's all connected to the Morning Star. You ought to hear the music on the other side of the gates!" she said.

"On the other side?" asked Castigio.

"Yes, everything is different there. This island is only the front side of the Kingdom. The other side has no end at all. We are still building," said Dreams.

Castigio cocked his head and thumped his helmet because he did not understand. Soot had stopped trying to figure it all out and was just enjoying her nectar, licking up the last drops.

"You mean the world is really flat after all and we could sail right off the edge one of these days?" asked Castigio.

"No," said Dreams. "You would reach one of the gates of the Kingdom first."

"You mean there are more than one?" asked Castigio.

"There are many, but only those who believe in the power of the Morning Star can get through," she said.

"What exactly is that power?" asked Castigio. He was certain he did not know.

"It's the power to make all things brand new! Even dead things!" said Dreams.

Castigio remembered the queer little ceremony he had seen in the basin of the gigantic fountain the first night he had seen the Kingdom. "I believe!" he said joyfully.

"Good!" said Dreams. "Then not even the fear of dying will stop you from fighting your way through to the gates. No one has ever come this far into these hills from the villages of this island, because they are too familiar with the tales of the dangers that lurk just outside the Kingdom gates. Once a merchant ventured near them and was attacked by gigantic buzzards. The people in the village below the mountain saw him being carried away. He was never seen again!

"There are other frightful tales about fiery dragons and murderous wolves who try to prevent everyone from getting into the Kingdom. Some tales are true and some not. It is the fear of confronting them that keeps people away. They are afraid of death," Dreams stopped and stared at Castigio. "Are you?" she asked at last.

"I always was before," he said. "But now it doesn't make sense that I should be, does it? Not if that same Star can do for me what I saw it do for that dead man the soldiers brought into the fountain."

"You saw that?" said Dreams and hopped down off her rock as if she were astonished at something.

"Yes!" Castigio said. "At least I did if it were not just a dream."

"That is one of our legends, Castigio. It is the story of the Shepherd who watches over these hills. He was murdered by an evil beast and brought back to life through the rays of the Bright Morning Star!"

"Could I possibly have met him?" wondered Castigio aloud as he recalled his strange encounter with a Shepherd.

"It happened thousands of years ago. Were you here thousands of years ago?"

"No, just a few days ago," said Castigio honestly.

"Then there is only one way that this could have happened for you," said the maiden thoughtfully.

"The Morning Star himself must have touched you! It was a vision, Castigio! You saw it with your eyes open, but it was a vision!" she exclaimed.

Castigio stood up and asked, "How do you know I didn't just dream it?"

"Because I am the keeper of dreams on this island. I know what all the dreams are made of," she explained. "I give them out at night on the wings of my songs when all the villagers have gone to bed. I sit up here on this hill above them and call them back home every morning before the villagers awake. If I did not do that, they would trample their dreams into the dust with their doubts and talk. The dreams would get twisted in the tasks the villagers do each day, and they would not appreciate them anymore. Some dreams would get lost! So I keep the dreams safe for the villagers up here."

"Where do the dreams go during the day?" Castigio asked.

"They are whisked away to the other side of the earth where it is dark now and men in China are sleeping," Dreams said.

"Really?" asked Castigio.

"Yes. Dreams are very useful things," answered Dreams. "But I have never given out a dream of something that happened in the past, only of things that could help in the future. I try to encourage men to believe their dreams so that they will be brave enough to journey on to the Kingdom of the Bright Morning Star. What has happened to you is very special Castigio."

Castigio blushed.

"Perhaps you can help me," said the maiden.

"How?" asked Castigio for he was eager to serve the lovely creature in any way he could.

"There is one village down there on the other side of a sea. I send my dreams there every evening, but they refuse to even mention the dreams in the day. It has always been so hard to get the villagers to believe in the dreams. Of late it has been even worse!"

"Why?" said Castigio compassionately. He did not like to see her pretty face grieved.

"An evil pirate has moved in there. He has made a decree against daydreaming. He doesn't want any of the villagers to leave the village, so he refuses to let them think of things that would make them want to go. He has cast a certain spell on them and will soon have them all as his slaves. The only kind of person whom he cannot rule is one who dares to dream!"

"I know the man!" shouted Castigio. Leaping up, he danced about with glee. It was clear to him how he, the greatest coward of all his shipmates, had been able to escape him. "He is El Capitan! And, bless the Morning Star, I am a dreamer! He said I was a fool! But I am not! I am a dreamer!"

"Oh, you are not a fool! You certainly are not! You are the exact sort of person I needed to find!" exclaimed the maiden joyfully. "This is a heavenly connection! Castigio, would you accept a commission in the service of the Morning Star for me?"

"Certainly! For that glorious Morning Star, yes!" exclaimed Castigio standing to attention at the mere mention of that name. It had such a marvelous effect on him.

"I thought so," said Dreams with a pleased smile. "I commission you in the name of the Morning Star to awaken the hearts of all who dwell in that village down there!" She pointed over the mountains to a place beyond the sea. "You will show them how to live out their dreams and find the Kingdom of the Morning Star!" Dreams was so excited that she piped a sparkly tune on her flute. A covey of doves in the glen twittered too, "You! You! You!"

"Who? Me?" choked Castigio.

"Yes! You Castigio!" said Dreams.

"What about the pirate? What can I do about him?" Castigio protested.

"He will have no power over you, Castigio, because you are a dreamer and he is a fool who does not believe in the power of dreams. You will escape his every plot. The Morning Star will guide you somehow. You will see!"

Castigio looked doubtful.

"Remember the Morning Star!" Dreams said encouragingly and piped another tune.

"Yes, the Morning Star!" Castigio suddenly heard himself exclaim. Oh! How strangely brave it always made him feel. Not only did his heart bubble with excitement, but his legs too began to dance to the lively marching tune that Dreams was playing. They felt as though they might run off to duty without him if he lingered in doubt any longer. It seemed as if his heart and body had answered the call in spite of his worrisome head. Castigio marveled as he found himself rejoicing in the face of danger.

Soot, who had been watching the two of them dance about finally spoke up, "Castigio, you ought to be ashamed of yourself, carrying on so happily when our friend Prince Zip is missing. We have no idea what misfortune has found him!"

"Oh," said Castigio somberly and stopped his dancing toes.

"What friend?" asked Dreams.

"We have a lion cub who has helped us along much of our way. He was here with us last evening. Now he is missing," explained Soot.

"Then let us look for him," said Dreams. She began to search about the clearing and sent all of the animals out looking too. At last she spoke up, "My cape is missing!"

"So it is," agreed the Spaniard.

"It is a sign," Dreams said. "I found that cape in an eagle's nest on the cliffs above the Kingdom gates. I knew that it did not belong there. So I picked it up to take it back to its rightful owners. I was going to take it to them today."

"Who are its rightful owners?" asked Soot.

"The Lions of the Royal Guard," she answered.

"Mercy sakes!" exclaimed Castigio. "That's where Prince Zip claims he was kidnapped from!"

"Then some worse foe has kidnapped him again, because none of the Lions would break rank to come out here alone in search of him," said Dreams shaking her head.

"Who could have done it?" asked Castigio.

"There is one evil creature who would delight in such mischief, although the creature would have no

"Is it Abaddon?" quivered the lamb, interrupting.

"Most likely so," said Dreams. "How do you know of him?"

"He has been chasing us for a while," said Soot.

"Then you had better hurry to find your friend. Abaddon has probably led him over to Tall Mountain on the other side of the sea to get him lost in the wilderness there," she told them pointing to the mountains.

"Stop in the village below it on your way through, and ask if they have seen him. And, remember, see what good you can do to mention me to them. Will you?"

"Oh, certainly!" they answered.

"How do we get out of here?" asked Soot.

"I'll guide you with my song," said Dreams and she headed for the stream at the edge of the clearing.

"Wait! Don't go so fast!" called Castigio after her. She flitted along ahead of them with her feet barely touching the ground. The song of her pipe sounded like running water and seemed to melt into one voice with the noises of the stream as they got closer to it. Dreams swished one of her skirts behind a flowering bush, and Castigio lost sight of her again.

"Wait for us, Dreams! We can't run so fast!" Castigio called. By the time they had climbed down the banks of the stream she was gone from sight.

"Where did she go?" asked Soot.

"It doesn't really matter, Soot. Can't you hear her song?" asked Castigio peacefully.

Soot listened and thought she could. "Is it the stream I hear or her flute?" she said at last.

"It's her song," said Castigio. Soot thought she understood as he began to skip through the stream toward the valley and she followed him.

## 13

## Battling the Sea Spirits

"Castigio, this water is getting too deep!" complained Soot, after they had waded through the stream for many miles. The water had reached her shoulders. "Can't we walk on the bank for a while before I drown?" she bleated.

Castigio had not noticed. He had been too busy listening to the sounds of the water, thinking about Dreams' lovely songs and all that she had told him about his vision. The water had drenched his bloomers and flooded his armor. Still he waded on into deeper waters.

"Castigio, are you listening to me?" asked the frustrated lamb once more.

"Oh, Soot, can't you swim?" he said absentmindedly looking back at her. "If you can't you'll surely drown that way."

"Of course I can swim. But I don't intend to swim all the way across this river!" she answered him sharply, pointing to the widening stream before them.

Castigio noticed how it had become a river.

"Dear me. I quite forgot you, Soot. I was so busy thinking about myself these last few hours," said Castigio.

"I noticed!" Soot snapped back.

"I hope you weren't offended by my silence," Castigio said as he helped her to the banks of the river.

"Only a little," she pouted, pleased that he had apologized.

"Mercy sakes, I hadn't noticed how deep that stream was getting," he said as he climbed out on the bank with her and surveyed it. Not far beyond them the river began to open up swiftly and empty into a clear blue sea.

"The Shepherd and Dreams both said we have to cross this sea to reach the village and the Tall Mountain behind it," said Castigio to the lamb.

"How are we going to do that?" asked Soot as she looked out across the water. The fishing villages on the other side were only tiny dots of color in the distance. They seemed so very far away.

"We'll have to hail a boat when one passes by," suggested the Spaniard.

"Castigio, haven't you noticed something odd about this place?" said Soot at last.

"What, Soot?" he asked.

"It's the middle of the day. Shouldn't there be fishing boats out there at this hour? Well, look how quiet it is. There's not one anywhere in sight," she said.

"That is odd, Soot. You seem to be right. I guess we won't find a ride today," Castigio replied.

"Do you think it's a holiday or something?" asked Soot.

"Um...I doubt if it's a holiday. From the way Dreams talked, it seemed that the people have to work too hard for that. No, Soot, I would rather fear that it's the 'something' that keeps them away and that worries me," Castigio said.

"What do you mean, Castigio?" she asked.

"Well, when I was at sea with the pirates, I often heard them talk of wild sea spirits that dwell in the depths. They are wicked and sly and will attack any ship whenever the notion strikes them!" said Castigio.

"You don't say!" shivered the lamb.

"Yes, I do!" said Castigio. "I wouldn't be a bit surprised if that is what had us off course the night my ship wrecked on this island's shores."

"Do you really believe in those fairy tales?" asked Soot.

"Unfortunately, I do," Castigio assured her. "As a matter of fact, I'll wager that there are some out there in those waters right now and that they are keeping sensible sailors away!" he said in a very convincing voice. "That's what worries me."

"Oh, Castigio, I wish you hadn't said that!" Soot told him. "We have to get across, and now I'm too scared."

Castigio realized that his choice of topics had not been well chosen. He began to wish he did not believe in such things either.

"Never mind, Soot," he said trying to console her and reassure himself. "If the Morning Star wants us to make it across, then there will be a way!" Just saying so made everything seem a little better.

Castigio and Soot kept walking until they came to the shores of the sea. What they saw there didn't make them feel any better, though. Lining the shore were the ghostly remains of many a sailing vessel. The ribs of a ship here and another there jutted out of the sand like a graveyard of shipwrecked sailors. It was an eerie sight.

Castigio and Soot walked along in silence not daring to speak their thoughts and fears to one another. It seemed that the screeching of sea spirits could be heard whistling through the tattered pieces of sails and rigging that lay about.

"This is a haunted place," whispered Castigio at last. "The sooner we get away from here the better." Soot agreed.

"What do you say we rope some of these scraps together and make a raft while it's still daylight? Then we can see where we're going. I certainly don't want to be here after dark!" said Castigio.

"Me either!" exclaimed Soot firmly.

They set to work salvaging pieces of deck, masts and sails. That kept them working until sundown roping it all together.

"There!" Castigio said at last dusting off his hands and picking up the sword. "I'll bet that you'll not find another raft more seaworthy than she!" he said proudly because he had never built anything else before and it looked just fine to him.

"It's wonderful!" said Soot admiringly.

"Let's shove off before dark!" said Castigio. He had looked toward the sky and had seen how low the sun had slipped as they stood there admiring his creation.

"Bon voyage!" he cried to Soot as they climbed aboard and pushed off from shore with a stick.

"What ever does that mean?" Soot asked.

"I haven't the foggiest notion, my friend. But sailors always say it for good luck. So I thought we should have it too," Castigio explained as best he could. Soot thought that was acceptable as she knew nothing of such affairs and trusted him completely.

The gentle lapping of the sea at the sides of the raft had begun to make Castigio seasick again. He had not made any oars and had thrown away the stick as soon as they were away from the shore. He knew of nothing else to do but to sit on the raft and wait until the tide carried them to the other side.

Castigio looked over at Soot and discovered that the raft had rocked her to sleep. So he decided he would rather be asleep too than seasick and tried to find a comfortable position to drift off. It wasn't easy, because he hadn't given any thought to that when he was building the raft. Finally he managed to prop his hands up on his sword and lay his head between his knees. He was just about to doze off when he thought he heard voices behind them.

"Swack-swack! We shall be nasty! Swack-swack! We shall be rude! Swack-swack! We shall be richer after this naughty feud!"

Castigio tried hard to tell himself he was imagining things, but he wasn't. It was the sea spirits that he had feared. They were wicked and sly, ready to live up to all that had been said about them! Without a breeze of warning, the mischievous phantoms were known to come upon a ship and stir up a fierce storm. Some would start up a howling screech of a wind, the kind that chills one's bones. Then the others would begin untying sailor's knots and tangling their sails. Stealing was their worst trick. They were so quick that they could even take the buckles off a sailor's shoes before he knew it! They had come to bother Castigio and Soot, because they had seen the golden sword in Castigio's hand, and they wanted it!

Castigio buried his head deeper in his knees and tried to get to sleep faster, as if that would erase the things he thought he had just imagined. But the wind began to howl louder and the sea grew choppy. He clutched his sword tighter and grit his teeth to keep them from chattering with fear.

The rough sea awakened Soot. She began to wail, "Castigio, what's happening? Are we going to sink? Save me!"

## Battling the Sea Spirits

Castigio knew they were going to be quite helpless against the full force of the sea spirits' attack when it would come. He did not know what to do except to hold on tight. "Hold onto me!" he yelled to the lamb. She did, and he clenched the sword so tight that his fist turned white. With the other hand he hugged her close. No sooner had he done this than the sea spirits sprang upon them. They couldn't see a thing but the sky grew darker and a wind blew around them so fast that it felt as if it meant to rip them apart.

Piece by piece, the raft began to come untied. Logs were breaking off. The waves drenched them both, tossing them high above the raft, then slapping them down again. They were barely recovering from their breath being knocked out of them when the sea tossed them up again.

"Oh! We're going to drown!" gasped the lamb.

"Just hang on tight!" yelled Castigio. "It can't go on forever!" He hoped he was right. Then as if to contradict him, the sea spirits began to chant, "Swack-swack! We shall be nasty! Swack-swack! We shall be rude! Swack-swack! We shall be richer after this naughty feud!"

"Castigio!" choked the lamb. "What do they want to make them richer?"

"I'm afraid it's my sword!" he yelled.

"Then for heaven's sake give it to them!" Soot said.

"Are you crazy, Soot? If we do that, we'll have nothing left to use in defending ourselves!"

"We don't know how to use it, anyway!" she reminded him. "Just give it to them, I say! Or, we'll not live to master it!"

When Castigio refused to hand the sword over to her, she kicked him hard with her hoof and knocked it from his hand. "Castigio, let them have it!" she screamed as it slipped over the side of the raft and splashed into the sea!

Just then the raft split completely apart, and Soot screamed for dear life as though she would drown. Castigio did not hear her for he had dived overboard the instant she had knocked his sword into the sea. He was already under the waves, diving like a fish as he watched the sword's jeweled handle sinking beneath him.

Suddenly, something caught him by the ankle and tossed him above the waves. For a second he caught a breath. Then it plunged him back down again just in time for him to see a scaly green coil wrap itself around the sword! A sea serpent had stolen it while the phantoms were busy wrestling for it up above.

Blowing bubbles out his nose, Castigio held his breath. *Mercy sakes alive!* he thought. *I just have to get my hands on it!* He reached out his hand and was only inches away when another coil of the serpent's body wrapped itself around his arm and tied about him in a knot.

Castigio began to feel faint as he ran out of air. And just when he thought he was going to drown for sure, he felt something pull him out of the serpent's grasp and toss him above the waves.

"Swack! Swack! Give it back!" screamed a spine tingling voice in his ear. It was a sea spirit!

# Battling the Sea Spirits

"I don't have it!" gasped Castigio.

Furiously, the sea spirit whipped himself into a whirlpool of rage and disappeared below to find the sword.

For an instant Castigio found himself thrown above the waters in the wake of the spirit's departure.

Gratefully he took another gulp of air before he plunged even deeper. This time he found the serpent engulfed in a furious bubbling, churning whirlpool as the invisible sea spirits discovered that the serpent had stolen their prize from them. The serpent's coils were releasing and Castigio found himself able to swim away. But just as he got free, something hard and cold fell past his hand. In the murky water he squinted to see what it was but couldn't make it out.

"Just grab it!" urged a voice deep inside his heart. And so he did! To Castigio's great amazement and joy, his hand closed around the jeweled handle of his sword. "Fight!" commanded the same little voice strongly. And he did indeed!

Castigio pulled the sword from its sheathe and began to slash it about blindly in the waves. Great chunks of scales and serpent went flying in every direction. The sea spirits fled and their stormy attack ceased as suddenly as it had begun. Before Castigio quite knew what had happened he was above the waves again. There, taking in deep breaths of salty air, he found himself drifting on a nice large chunk of wood. His sword was safe in its sheathe once more, held tight in his fist. And floating beside him was the weary lamb.

"What happened Castigio?" she asked weakly and then passed out on top of her board.

Great chunks of scales and serpent went
flying in every direction.

"I hardly think I know," Castigio said with wonder. He marveled at the power of the sword once again. Then he drifted off to sleep in the rocking waves determining he would have to spend more time learning how to use it when he got the chance.

## 14

# Kidnapped!

Throughout the night Castigio and Soot drifted on top of the wreckage of their raft. A moonbeam shone brightly across their backs, as it pulled the tide toward the shore of the fishing village. Neither awoke till morning. The battle had worn them out. It was as if some unseen hand were guiding them again.

"Crack!" Castigio awoke with a jerk! He grabbed for his sword, then realized he was still clenching it tightly in his other hand. He had almost lost it twice on the journey. He was not about to lose it again. Looking around, he saw that his log had bumped into some sort of pier.

Castigio sat up in a dazed state of mind. He tried to figure out where he was. For the moment he could only recall his dreams of the night before. He did not immediately remember the sea spirits' battle or how he had floated to this harbor. He looked around, squinting his eyes for the brightness of the morning sun dancing on the water. Then he saw a familiar sight drifting toward him.

"Soot!" he called excitedly and reached out to catch her. It was then he remembered their battle at sea.

"Castigio?" she said sleepily peeping up at him as she stiffly opened one eye. "What happened to our wonderful raft?"

"Don't you remember how the sea spirits attacked us last night?" Castigio asked as he pulled her floating piece of wreckage to him.

"Oh! Yes! Now I do!" she said, wet and shivering in the cool morning breeze.

"I guess we got 'bon voyage!'" she said.

"We got what?" Castigio asked.

"Bon voyage! You said it for good luck. Didn't you? It was a good thing you did, I guess, because we had good luck to still be alive!" reasoned the lamb.

"So we did!" Castigio agreed.

"Castigio, where do you suppose we are?" asked Soot as she sat up on her board and began to fluff out her white fleece in the sunshine. It felt so good!

"I'm not sure I can tell you, Lambkin," he said slipping off the other side of his log as he tried to climb out of the water too. He had not been fortunate to cling to as large a piece of wreckage as hers. So he found himself stuck in the water. He had to be content to drift along toward shore with just his head and sword showing above the surface. It made him feel just like a shriveled up old prune as his suit and britches were completely water logged and sagged in heavy wrinkles beneath him.

Castigio looked around. They were in some sort of port. Soot also noticed boats bobbing up and down on the water nearby. Curiously they looked for signs of life.

"It seems we have landed under a pier of sorts, Soot!" said Castigio.

"Yes, and it must be a safer place than on the other side of the sea, because there are lots of boats tied to it. That means people can sail around here. No more sea spirits!" she said happily. "We are out of danger!"

Castigio listened to her conclusions as he eyed the port cautiously. The thought of being around people again began to make him nervous, especially because he did not know what kind of people they were.

"Let's find a way to get to shore!" Soot said.

"No, Soot! Wait!" he cautioned her. "Let's stay under the shadow of this pier until we can investigate a little. No sense in jumping out of the soup into the fire, is there?" Castigio asked her.

"What are you talking about?" Soot asked.

"I mean, the sea spirits were bad enough. But some people can be worse," the Spaniard said. "Let's wait to see what kind of sailors come out to get their boats. They should be arriving soon to check their nets. If they are nice fellows, we can ask for their help."

Soot agreed and kept a sharp eye open from her perch on top of the wreckage as Castigio held on to it and paddled them along with his feet under the shadows of the pier.

"Do you think we will find Prince Zip here?" she asked.

"I hope so, Soot. If this is where Abaddon took him, then we will have a good chance to rescue him," Castigio answered.

"How will we do that?" Soot asked swinging herself out into a sunny spot, where light shone down on the water through a crack in the boards of the pier above. She was determined to get a little of the sunshine each time they passed under a crack, because she did not like staying in the shadows.

Castigio pulled her back again and said, "You mean rescue him?"

"Yes. Do you have any ideas of how to...," she was about to say 'rescue him' when she passed under another crack and swung away from Castigio's grip again. "Rescue me!" Soot bleated!

"You?" gasped the startled Spaniard. Castigio looked up just in time to see the lamb's feet disappearing from sight as someone whisked her up in a net above the pier.

He heard a gruff voice saying, "Trying to escape were ye?" and then Soot calling for help, "Oh, my hoofs and curls! My hoofs and curls! Castigio, help me! I've been kidnapped!"

"Kidnapped! Oh, no!" cried the little Spaniard.

"Castigio, help me! I've been kidnapped," the lamb cried.

"Mercy sakes! First Prince Zip and now you too?" he said, "What's a fellow to do?" He moved back along the banks of the pier into the darkest part of the shadows until the heavy footsteps of Soot's captors had crossed the last board above. Then he waited a few minutes more to be sure he would not be discovered and cautiously waded out onto the bank.

The bank was slimy and covered with seaweed and barnacles just like the bilge of his old ship. He was used to slipping and sliding on such things, so when he thought it safe to come out at last, he did not let the slippery bank slow him down much. He was fast getting to the top side of the pier.

Castigio popped his head up above the pier just in time to see the coattails of a husky sailor disappear around the corner of a street leading away from the pier. "The kidnapper!" Castigio said to himself.

"What to do? What to do?" He looked around to see if he was being watched, then ran down the same cobblestone street after the sailor, his armor sloshing as he went.

Turning the corner was a great disappointment, for the kidnapper had already vanished into a doorway of one of the many rough little houses that lined the street. Castigio did not know what to do. Walking a little ways, he came to a stone well in the center of a plaza where many more streets joined together. They made him the more baffled. He turned in circles not knowing which one could lead to the kidnapper.

Castigio heard a door on one of the streets open and slam. He hid under a bench near the well. There he listened for footsteps, but the ones he heard faded off in the distance, away from the direction of the pier.

# Kidnapped!

By and by he heard another door open and slam. Someone was putting on wooden shoes and banging fishing poles and buckets together. He came down the street. Castigio peered out from under the bench to see. It was just a fisherman going off to check his nets at the dock. Castigio decided that he was not husky enough to be the kidnapper.

The streets were quiet at that early hour of the morning except for the occasional slamming of a door here and there and the clattering of wooden shoes as other fishermen crept out of their houses to set to work in the port.

Castigio stayed under the bench, listening. At last he decided to consult the echo in his helmet for some idea of what he might do to rescue the lion or the lamb. It had always been a handy device before when he had been in a tight spot, and an acceptable companion for loneliness. He scrunched up his shoulders and ducked into the space of the helmet.

This time it did not seem to fit just right. It was too tight and would not slide easily over his nose as before. Castigio wondered if the angel food had made him too fat for it all of a sudden. He tried to speak his thoughts out loud in it anyway.

"Soot is lost, and Prince Zip too. Oh, faithful echo, tell me what to do!" he pleaded.

"..."

To his astonishment there was no reply at all! Castigio could not believe it. For years he had been so accustomed to taking counsel from his own thoughts with the help of the echo, that he just could not understand the problem! "This has never happened before!" he said. Again there was no echo.

Fumbling, Castigio pushed the helmet over his ears and took it off.

"My trusty, rusty helmet, where did your echo go?" he asked it, blinking back a tear.

"Into the Pilgrim soup!" replied a voice deep within his heart.

"Oh, say it isn't so!" Castigio groaned at the thought of it. "Did you say so truly?" he asked the voice. There was no reply. Castigio was not used to listening to the voice of his own heart. He had preferred to reason with his head and the echo for all those years. He was not certain if he was going to like it much. It would take some getting used to. The voice of his heart was not one to be changed around as the silly little echo had been. When it said something, it was final.

Sadly, Castigio tossed the helmet about in his lap and realized that the voice of his heart was true. It had been leading him more and more since he had met the Morning Star. It had always been right thus far. Then he remembered how the nasty little Pilgrim had snatched his helmet from his head and mistaken it for a turtle shell. Castigio had replaced it with this one from the Pilgrim's trunk.

"Cooked in a soup! What a hard way to be retired!" Castigio sighed for he was like many others who get attached to habits and things. It is painful to let them go sometimes even when we know we must.

Thus, for a time, Castigio lost himself in sorrowful thoughts about the trusty helmet and Soot his faithful friend.

15

# Vanity Fair

The town and village plaza were waking up all around Castigio. But he had not noticed because of his moment of grieving. He was still sitting under the bench when a small boy about eight years old found him there.

Pit-Ting!

"What the?" Castigio looked up. Something had ricocheted off his helmet.

Pit-ting! Sting! A pebble hit the helmet again and glanced off his arm.

"Ouch!" cried Castigio. He heard childish laughter and looked around the well to see a mean little boy shooting rocks with a slingshot at him from the other side.

"Hey, young fellah! Stop that!" scolded Castigio, "You're going to hurt somebody with that thing!" he said as he dived under a bush near the bench for cover.

"That's the idea!" said the mean child, taking aim again.

"You'd better stop that, or I'll find your mother and tell her what you've been up to here!" Castigio threatened, even though, of course, he didn't know the boy's mother.

"I haven't got one!" sneered the naughty boy. "I'm an orphan!"

"Oh, no, not another one!" Castigio thought aloud as he was reminded of all the mischief Prince Zip had gotten into, because he was an orphan.

"You'd better not let anyone else catch you daydreaming here so lazy!" said the boy as he shot off another clump of pebbles at the Spaniard.

"Why not?" asked Castigio ducking just in time as they shot past his head.

"We've got a law against it!" said the boy as he changed positions behind the well. Castigio could not see how to hide from him now, so he listened for the bragging voice, "Peddlers and shoppers will be coming out soon to start the day and after that, as fast as a jack rabbit blinks one eye, you can be sure the dreamsnatchers and the beasts will be passing by too!"

Castigio remembered what the maiden on the hill had told him about the village El Capitan had sieged and about how he had passed such a law. "Say, you haven't seen a pirate in these parts, have you?" said Castigio.

"Yes, sir, and he lives right here!" said the mean little boy. "And I just might catch you for him!" he said, sneaking up on Castigio from behind the bush. "Then we'll have a banishing today, and that will be exciting!"

"What is a banishing?" Castigio asked, all the while wondering if there could ever be another pirate as evil as El Capitan.

"If the dream-snatchers catch you breaking the law, they string you up from the top of this well and make a spectacle of you for everyone to see. Then they cut you down and banish you into exile on a glacier up there in them mountains! Then the wild beasts get you, and it's all over!" said the boy.

"And you'd like to see them do that to me?" asked Castigio nervously.

"Not actually," said the child. "But I enjoy the crowds at a good banishing! It's the best time to pick their pockets and take my meals from their carts!"

Castigio felt sorry for him, because he knew what it was like to be hungry sometimes. "Listen!" Castigio coaxed him as he struggled to see where the boy would shoot from next, "Be a good lad and make a deal with me!"

"What kind of deal?" asked the boy with interest.

"I have something with me that no one in this village has ever seen before. It's a magic sword with special power. I'll let you look at it, if we can call a truce and be friends!"

There was a moment of silence from the boy. Castigio listened and could hear busy street sounds from around the plaza, but not from the boy. It made him a little nervous again as he waited for an answer.

Pit-ting-ting-ting! came the reply as a spray of pebbles hit Castigio's helmet and rolled down his neck.

"Ouch!" exclaimed Castigio looking around.

"Lucky thing I and not the dream-snatchers found you first!" said the boy popping his head through the top of the bush.

"Lucky thing," muttered Castigio as he rubbed his neck from the sting of the pebbles. "Does this mean you have decided to be friends?"

"Depends on what you have to show me!" said the eager child as he climbed through the bush.

"No, it doesn't," said Castigio wisely. "First we call a truce, and then you see it."

"What's a truce?" asked the boy, taking aim at close range with the slingshot.

Castigio reached out and snatched it away quickly.

"Hey, gi'me back!" screamed the mean little boy.

"A truce means you stop shooting at me, and we put our weapons aside and act like respectable friends!" said Castigio holding the slingshot hostage. The child saw that he had no other choice and dropped his hands by his side in surrender

Castigio stood up and looked the boy over once or twice to see if he could be trusted with the sword. It was a gamble, but he certainly did not wish to be turned in for banishing. At least not until he found Soot and Prince Zip.

"Are you a man or a dwarf?" quizzed the child rudely, just as Castigio had almost decided to let him look at the sword.

"None of your business!" said Castigio as he pulled the sword away with a second thought. "Are you a little boy or a beast?" he added.

"A little boy, of course!" said the child. "Oh, please let me see your sword. I'll be good! You promised!" he begged.

Castigio looked at his dirty face and tattered clothes. He felt sorry for him again as he stood there pleading with two excited brown eyes that seemed to take up his whole face.

"Tell me your name first," said Castigio as he began to hold out the sword again.

"Fetch-it!" said the boy. He reached out and grabbed the sword quick as lightning. "Wow! This is a true treasure. How many creatures could you whip with this?" he said drooling with excitement as he flipped the precious sword over in his hands.

"A good many I suppose, but tell me, is Fetch-it really your name?" asked Castigio keeping a close eye on him.

"Sure is! That's all anybody ever says to me. I run errands sometimes for a baker and other times for a butcher and once in a while for a peddler or two. And they always say 'Fetch it here or Fetch it there,' and they pay me. So whenever anybody needs an errand boy they call for Fetch-it and I come running. It's a

"Are you a man or a dwarf?" quizzed the child.

good way to eat," the boy explained. "Say, have you killed any monsters with this yet?"

"Yes! A serpent just yesterday!" said Castigio proudly. He was very glad it had happened, for just then it was exactly the thing he needed to say to get the boy's attention and respect.

"Wow! Are you a brave warrior or something?" asked Fetch-it respectfully.

Castigio yanked the sword away. He was concerned about letting the boy get too attached to it. Then he waved it in the air with a brave gesture and pretended to know a lot about it as if he had always held it so.

"You might say so!" he replied.

"Oh! I'd sure like to go on an adventure with you!" offered the boy.

"I thought you were going to banish me!" said Castigio testing him.

"Naw! That was just for some excitement. But this would be better," Fetch-it said trying to get another look at the sword.

"Maybe there's a law against that too! Don't adventures kind of fall into the same category as dreams?" asked Castigio. He wasn't sure he wanted to take such a fickle companion along with him.

"I don't follow those silly old laws anyway," bragged Fetch-it. "I'm too fast for the beasts when I break them. I'm good at hiding."

"Oh, so am I," said Castigio. He was beginning to like this mischievous boy a little better already because he could tell that Fetch-it was a dreamer just like he was.

"Say, are you some kind of a knight or somethin'?" asked the boy as he touched the carving on the sword again and ran his fingers down the sheathe. "You are! I bet! Aren't you?" he said looking at Castigio's armor.

"You might say so!" bragged Castigio.

"What kingdom are you from? Somewhere far away on the other side of the world?" Fetch-it begged to know.

"I'm on a secret mission from the Kingdom of the Morning Star!" said Castigio, marveling at how important that sounded. "Have you ever heard of it, young fellow?"

"Have I ever!" said Fetch-it. His childish eyes popped open wider with excitement. "Why, that's what all the fuss is about around here. Some folks say there is such a place behind Tall Mountain and the rest say it's just a fairy-tale place. I like to dream about it and imagine what it would be like to go there someday. But I sure never met anybody who's been there!"

"It's a real place, and I'm going back!" said Castigio confidently.

"Oh, take me with you! Ple-ease!" begged the boy. "Nobody will miss me here. I can be your errand boy!"

"We'll see," said Castigio as he wasn't sure that he could handle Fetch-it and Prince Zip both.

"First I have to find somebody," he said.

"Who? The pirate? Did you come to rescue everybody from him and the dream-snatchers? If you could do that, then we would all be free to dream again. And lots of people would believe in that place. It's a regular prison to grow up here in a village where no one will let you dream! Just awful!" pleaded the child.

Castigio was moved with compassion for him again as he could remember El Capitan making him feel like a fool for the same crime. "Is that why you shot me with your sling?" he asked.

"Oh, yes! I was so bored. I took you for a bum. It looked like a fun way to get through the morning till the merchants open up the shops," confessed Fetch-it.

"What's this pirate's name?" Castigio went on.

"El Capitan!" whispered the boy.

"I thought so!" exclaimed Castigio, and then he was positive he had come to the right village of which Dreams had told him and was on the right path of which the Shepherd had spoken.

"You know him?" asked the boy in astonishment.

"Yes. What is a dream-snatcher?" Castigio asked.

The boy was about to answer when a terrible commotion on the plaza and the streets interrupted them.

"They're here!" Fetch-it yelled and pushed Castigio under the bushes with him. From there he watched in amazement at all that was taking place around them.

Everyone in the streets was scurrying away in a panic! Roasted pigs in the butcher shop window swallowed their apple stuffings. Rats even fled from their garbage feasts. Fishermen at the end of the pier fished faster and peddlers sold their wares louder!

Cobblers tick-tacked the heels of their shoes quicker, and shoeshine boys shined them brighter. They had all become very, very busy! No one wanted to be accused of daydreaming!

"What's happening?" demanded Castigio.

"Shh!" said the frightened boy.

Castigio then heard the tromping of many feet like the sound of an army. The ground shook, and a familiar shadow passed by. It looked like a giant rhinoceros. He recognized it to be none other than that of El Capitan! By his side was a snarling black beast that he recognized to be Abaddon. El Capitan had him on a leash! But Castigio could not really tell who was leading whom! Following behind were some of the meanest sailors from his old ship. Each was fitted with a spiked helmet like El Capitan's and carried a barbed spear. After them rolled a caravan of brightly painted cages on carts. In each one was some ferocious beast: a wolf or hyena, a bear or a wildcat. Each was showing off its vicious teeth in the vainest style.

"The dream-snatchers!" breathed Fetch-it. "If the pirate catches anybody daydreaming or trying to escape the village, he turns them over to the dream-snatchers when they are banished!"

"I knew he was wicked before. But he's gotten worse!" Castigio said as he marveled at the terrifying sight. Then he realized it must have been the power of the Morning Star that had helped him escape El Capitan before. He could think of no other explanation.

The ground shook as a familiar shadow passed by.

Castigio watched as the evil troop turned down a corner and was followed by the trail of carts and cages. When the last one passed by he almost fainted with shock. For there, riding inside it like a king was the latest addition, Prince Zip!

He never even noticed what was going on about him but seemed very content to be in the parade with all eyes upon him.

"Your Majesty!" cried Castigio.

"Shh!" scolded the boy. "They'll hear you!"

"There's Prince Zip!" whispered Castigio

"A friend of yours with them?" asked the boy suspiciously cowering back as if he might run from Castigio at any moment.

"Yes, but he doesn't belong there! He's just a cub! He doesn't know what he's doing. He's just proud to be there. They've tricked him! It's just a vanity fair!" explained Castigio. "We've got to get him out of that cage!" he said, starting to get up.

"Well, I'm certainly not going to let you get us banished!" said Fetch-it yanking his slingshot free from Castigio's bloomers, where Castigio had hidden it. In an instant he had it loaded and let a pebble fly! It hit Castigio in the back and made him stop in his tracks to duck down.

"They're shooting something at us!" he said.

"No, they're not. But they might if you try that again!" warned the boy. "It was just me! Get back down here under these bushes, or they'll arrest us both. Castigio joined him once more.

Fetch-it waited until the last cage and cart had disappeared around a corner, then he sat up to wipe his brow with relief. "Wow! That was close!" he sighed.

Castigio looked at him and said, "I thought you told me that you weren't afraid of the dream-snatchers!"

"Most times not! But you almost got us both banished. What's the good of hiding here, if you give us away?" snapped the boy.

"Mercy me. I didn't think," said Castigio absentmindedly. "I'm sorry Fetch-it. It's just that my little friend was kidnapped, and now that I've found him, he's in great trouble!"

Fetch-it looked up with interest, "You mean busting him out of there could be an adventure?"

"Well, yes, if you put it like that! I suppose that it might be," said the Spaniard thoughtfully. "But I hope not," he added as he would rather not meet El Capitan or Abaddon again, if it could be helped.

"Well! What are we waiting for?" said Fetch-it enthusiastically as he grabbed the sword from Castigio.

"Hold on there!" yelled Castigio. Quickly he snatched it back and tucked it inside his bloomers for safekeeping, being careful to guard it tighter with one hand. "There's too much power in this thing for one little boy!"

"Well, couldn't you give me fightin' lessons? I catch on real quick!" begged the boy earnestly.

"Later," Castigio replied, not being certain how to really use it himself. The battle with the sea spirits had taken him by surprise. He felt that the sword had almost fought the battle all by itself. "Do you know where El Capitan keeps those cages?" he asked, changing the subject.

"Sure!" replied the boy. "He keeps them in a big circus tent near the docks."

"Why there?" asked Castigio.

"That's where he ships the beasts in and out of the village."

"That can't have been going on long," mused Castigio because he knew that the pirate had not been on the island longer than he.

"It's been going on for years!" said Fetch-it.

"Don't you fib to me, young fellow!" said Castigio, "I'll not take you on any adventure! Now tell the truth! I came to this island when the pirate did! It was just a few days ago!"

Fetch-it looked hurt as if he had been wrongfully accused of telling fibs.

"What's the matter? Cat got your tongue?" said Castigio. "Speak up, boy!"

"I told the truth!" insisted Fetch-it. "I wouldn't lie to a knight!"

"You wouldn't?" asked Castigio.

"No!" said the child. "Say, you're an old man, you know! Don't you think you could have forgotten how long ago you got here?"

"Knights never forget anything!" said Castigio defensively. He didn't want to lose respect so fast. Then, giving the situation a second thought, he asked, "How many years?"

"Oh, as long as I've been around," said Fetch-it.

Castigio poked his nose down in the boy's face to see if he was honest. He decided that the child seemed to be telling the truth. "I don't understand it at all!" said Castigio shaking his head. He walked over to the well and looked down into the water at the bottom hoping to find his reflection. He saw it in the dark pool and was surprised to see how white and how long his mustache had grown. "Something has happened to me!" he exclaimed. "I've gotten too old!"

"Too old for adventures?" asked Fetch-it.

"Just too old!" said Castigio in confusion. He tried to think of how age could have crept up on him so suddenly. "Maybe it was on that mountain where I saw the vision? Or, maybe it was in that cave where we took our cat nap or on the hill where Dreams found us? How long did I sleep?" he said. "Fetch-it, how long are the days here?"

The boy stopped to think, "Six hours," he answered.

"Six? That's all?" gasped the Spaniard.

"That's all. Aren't they the same where you come from?" asked the child wonderingly.

"No, they're much longer! Oh, mercy sakes, I'm confused! Something has happened to me here. This island is such a strange place!" He wondered if the Star had also altered time for him, as well as the other mysterious things that had happened to him since their first encounter.

"How old are you?" asked the child. He did not know any better than to be so rude.

"It's too hard to figure," said Castigio. "Just old I guess. If time passes so quickly here, then there is not a moment more to lose. We must find my friend right away!"

"We'd better find him before the pirates ship him out!" said Fetch-it in agreement.

"Ship him out?" asked Castigio. "I thought you said that the dream-snatchers kept the beasts in cages to release on the mountain at a banishing!"

"They do, some of them. But the most unusual ones get shipped out to some other place for lots of money. It's a big business. The pirates catch them here and send them there."

"Where?"

"I don't know," said Fetch-it.

"We have to hurry then. Take me to the circus tent, so we can help the cub escape before it's too late!" said Castigio.

Fetch-it looked around the plaza to see if all the coast was clear to come out of hiding. He decided that it was, as everyone had gone back to shopping and selling their wares by this time. "Come on!" he said. "No one will notice us now. We'll just mix in with the crowds till we get to the docks."

Castigio followed him out of the bushes just as a plump woman came to the well with her pitchers to fill. She set the pitchers down and watched Castigio and Fetch-it as they crawled on their bellies through the bushes to the street. When they had disappeared, she ran ahead of them down an alley and slipped into a tavern, looking over her shoulder to be sure they hadn't noticed her spying on them.

16

# An Adventure

**W**hen Castigio and Fetch-it had come to the end of the plaza and run out of crowd in which to hide, they straightened up their backs and pretended to look as if they were about their daily business like anyone else.

"Let's take this short cut to the docks," said Fetch-it, pointing down an alley. Castigio followed.

They were almost to the docks when a great wooden door swung open into their path from a building they were passing. Castigio had no time to step back, ran right into it and fell. Fetch-it tried to run around it, but bumped into someone coming out.

"It's them! The daydreamers I was telling you about!" shrieked a woman. It was the same one who had seen them leaving the well. She reached out to catch Fetch-it by the collar but missed as he wriggled away. "It's that orphan!" she screamed.

"Let's get out of here!" cried Fetch-it. "Come on!" He pushed Castigio to his feet. They took off as fast as they could with the woman yelling behind them, "Banish them! Banish them! Banish them!"

They heard the stomping of feet and the clatter of armor as the dream-snatchers ran out of the tavern after them.

"Quick! We can hide in here till they lose our trail!" said Fetch-it pointing the way to a butcher's shop. Castigio followed him from the alley through the backdoor. There, they ducked into a pile of burlap sacks and pretended to be two bagged hams.

Castigio panted to catch his breath and listened to see if the pirates would come in after them. There was silence. Still he waited, barely daring to breathe. Fetch-it did the same. When at last it seemed as if no one had seen them duck in there, Fetch-it spoke up.

"I think it's safe to come out now," he whispered.

Castigio climbed out of the sack and looked around. "What kind of a shop is this?" he asked sniffing the air, because it smelled smoky.

"It's a butcher shop," Fetch-it replied. I knew we'd be safe here because I fetch things for the butcher sometimes. There's lots of nooks and crannies in here. It's a good hidin' place!"

"What kinds of beasts does he butcher?" asked Castigio.

"Oh, pigs and lambs and...."

## An Adventure

"Lambs?" cried Castigio. "Oh, no! Soot! Am I too late?" he wailed.

"Who is Soot?" asked the boy.

"My other friend who was kidnapped too!" answered Castigio.

"You certainly don't keep them very well!" observed Fetch-it.

"Keep what?" asked Castigio.

"Your friends!" remarked the boy.

Castigio nodded his head sadly in agreement.

"Was this friend a lion too?" asked Fetch-it.

"No," replied Castigio solemnly. "She is a lamb – was. Or *is*, I hope!" He looked around at all the meat smoking as it hung from the ceiling.

"Who kidnapped her?" asked Fetch-it.

"A man on the pier!" said Castigio.

"When?"

"Only this morning!" sobbed Castigio mournfully.

"Then maybe she is still alive!" offered the child hopefully.

"Mercy sakes! I hope so! I was looking for her when I came to the well where you and I met," Castigio explained. He was about to go on when they heard a noise. Someone was coming into the smoke room from the front of the shop.

"Hide!" commanded Fetch-it, and they ducked back into the burlap sacks.

249

Two men came into the room carrying a load of wood. Castigio and Fetch-it could hear every word they said.

"Put that wood on the fire and help me pick up the rest of these hams. We've got to get them ready to deliver to the tavern for evening meals tonight. The cook has put in a large order. You know what we'll get if it's not filled on time!"

"Which ones do you want me to smoke?"

"All of them!"

Castigio heard their footsteps coming closer. Then he heard them picking up hams and burlap sacks. *Mercy sakes alive!* he thought. *We're going to be roasted and toasted and smoked!* No sooner had he thought it than was he hoisted into the air on a hook and hung in his sack from the ceiling.

"That last one was unusually heavy!" said one of the men.

"Good!" said the other, "That should make up for the order being a bit late!"

Castigio began to panic. Sweat poured down his face. The aroma of hickory smoke tickled his nose as it came through the bag. He wondered where they had hung Fetch-it. He had no idea how they would get themselves down again.

Castigio hadn't had time to worry about it when the shop door swung open and a heavy pair of feet stomped into the room followed by several others. Castigio could hear the clanking of armor. He wondered if the dream-snatchers had caught up to them after all.

## An Adventure

He was tempted to say, "Things are getting worse and worse," but decided he needed all the hope he could muster that they weren't. So instead he strained to listen.

"El Capitan!" gasped one of the men.

"Sir!" exclaimed the other.

"Have ye seen any loafers around here?" Castigio recognized the demanding, booming voice.

"No! No! We've been busy, as busy as two beavers putting up these hams!"

"We haven't seen any around here!"

"Ye didn't see that orphan, Fetch-it, hiding around here?" quizzed El Capitan sharply.

"No, sir! We didn't have any errands for him today," said one of the men nervously.

"Well, next time ye see him, nab him! He's a day-dreamer and a loafer. I'm going to banish him when I catch him. Better to get rid of him now than when he's grown up into a full-fledged troublemaker!" snarled the pirate viciously. Fetch-it gulped to hear his fate declared. He held his breath and hoped for the best until he could find an escape.

As El Capitan searched about, there was silence for a moment until he was satisfied that the men had told him the truth. On his way out the door he said, "They probably ran to hide under the docks!"

Castigio listened as some of the other feet began to follow the heavy feet of El Capitan out the door. Castigio heard the two butchers sigh in relief and he relaxed. It was a mistake, for just then a whiff of smoke tickled his nose and caught him off guard. He sneezed!

In a flash the dream-snatchers were back! They had not all left. The last one closing the door called for El Capitan to return. Castigio thought he might faint from fear as he heard El Capitan speak again.

"What's in those sacks up there?" he demanded.

"Hams, sir!" one of the men quickly responded. The butchers were afraid they would be accused of hiding criminals even though they had known nothing of it.

"To whom are you delivering them?" demanded the pirate.

"The tavern, sir!"

"For my dinner, I see?" said El Capitan greedily. "Ye won't mind then if I inspect them before my cook does. I wouldn't want anyone to have poisoned them. Would ye?" he snapped.

"Oh, no, sir! Certainly not!" said one of the men.

The other jumped in with a quick remark too, because he did not want the dream-snatchers to find whoever was hiding in them. "There's no need to inspect them, sir. The cook has already picked them out. We only sell the best! Anything served to you at the tavern we would eat on our own table!"

El Capitan did not seem convinced. Castigio and Fetch-it both listened anxiously.

"I'll just see for myself!" he growled and with that slashed open the bottom of a sack. A fat juicy ham fell out, ker-plunk, on the floor.

## An Adventure

"See!" laughed one of the men nervously. "I told you they were the best."

"I'll just inspect them all myself!" El Capitan sneered. "Ye seem too eager to convince me!" With that he slashed open another and another. Castigio listened to the hams hitting the floor. Ker-plunk! Ker-plunk! Ker-plunk! He tried to think fast and come up with a plan of escape when El Capitan would slash open his sack. *Maybe the Morning Star will help me again!* he thought. As he did, he heard a thud instead of a ker-plunk. It was Fetch-it!

El Capitan was so startled that he stopped slashing sacks. The boy made a beeline for the alley door and escaped them all. Castigio heard suits of armor crashing into each other from the chaos that followed as the pirate and the dream-snatchers gave chase to catch him. He heard them collide in the doorway at once, and it took them a few moments to squeeze through.

"Out of my way, ye fools!" the pirate was screaming.

"Quick! Let's run for our lives while we still can!" yelled one of the butchers to the other.

"Hurry before he comes back to banish us for hiding the little rascal!" said the other.

"I'll kill him myself, if they don't catch him first!" said the first man, as they fled through the front door of the shop.

Castigio was all alone again. *Poor Fetch-it!* he thought and pitied anyone who had become the

"Out of my way, ye fools!" the pirate screamed.

## An Adventure

object of El Capitan's wrath. He need not have worried, though, for the little boy was feisty enough to handle himself.

Castigio did not waste time thinking about Fetch-it too long either. He felt certain the pirate would return any minute with or without Fetch-it to punish the butchers.

"I've got to get out of here!" he said to himself. "Have mercy on me, Morning Star." Then he remembered his sword. "Tickle my whiskers, old fool!" he laughed. "Why didn't you think of this before!" With delight he pulled the sword from the sheathe and slashed open the bottom of his sack.

In an instant he landed on the floor. It was a rough exit, but he was glad to be free. The alley door was right beside the spot where they had hung him. So he picked himself up and headed out as fast as his old legs would carry him.

No sooner had he rounded a corner on the street than he heard the pirate and the dream-snatchers returning.

"Banish the butchers!" they were shouting. "The rascal got away, but they will pay!"

Castigio looked for a place to hide again. He heard lambs bleating and hogs snorting behind him and turned to see the butcher's holding pens. "They won't think to look here!" he exclaimed and crawled over the fence in the nick of time as the angry group stormed by. He was relieved to hear that Fetch-it got away, but felt sorry for the butchers.

"Get out of my trough!" scolded a muddy pig. Castigio had backed into her trough as he had tried to get down low in the pen to not be seen.

"Excuse me!" he apologized.

"Look where you're going!" squealed another pig as he turned around and fell over her back.

"Why don't you find another pen!" suggested a great hog as it stuck its nose down in his face while Castigio lay on his back trying to get up.

"Where?" asked Castigio very flustered.

"Over there with the sheep!" said a piglet as it darted between his legs.

Castigio climbed over the fence and landed in the sheep pen, hoping to be better received.

"Castigio?" said a little voice in surprise.

"Soot!" exclaimed the Spaniard. "You're alive!" How he rejoiced to see his friend!

"Yes! You came in time! They were going to butcher us all!" sobbed the lamb.

Castigio picked her up and hugged her tight. "I know and they almost roasted me for dinner!" he said.

"How did you find me?" Soot asked.

"It's too long a story to tell you now," he said, "We've got to figure out a way to get out of here before El Capitan finds us. I found Prince Zip, and we've got to rescue him too!"

"Where did you see him?" asked Soot.

"He's in a vanity fair of exotic animals. They are all in carnival cages in a circus tent near the docks."

"Look where you're going!" squealed a pig.

"What's he doing there?" asked the lamb.

"Abaddon tricked him into believing that he's a special attraction, it seems. But really, he's gotten himself trapped into a cage that will be sold on the docks and shipped away!"

"Is Abaddon here too?" shivered the lamb.

"Yes! But don't worry about that, Soot. It appears that his evil fortune has caught up with him at last. Somehow the pirates have captured him too!"

"Oh, it serves him right!" cheered the lamb.

"Let me see if I can tell whether or not the street is clear for us to make a run for it!" Castigio said as he started to climb up over the fence.

"Wait! I can't go with you Castigio!" Soot called.

"Lambkin, don't be silly, why not?" asked Castigio.

"Because I found my flock here! The Shepherd left them with his friends while he went out searching for me and some hireling kidnapped them all one night and brought them here to sell to the butchers."

"Is that why they captured you this morning?" Castigio guessed.

"Yes! They thought I was part of the flock trying to escape. They brought me here," Soot explained.

"Where are the kidnappers now?" asked Castigio.

"They are all in the tavern getting drunk," said the lamb.

"Good! Then I'll open the gate and let us all go free!" said the Spaniard. He climbed up and looked around. Then he slipped the pin out of the latch and opened the gate! "Go home! You're free!" he yelled.

# An Adventure

The sheep stampeded out of the pen as he scrambled up on the fence. "Soot, aren't you going to follow your flock?" he asked sadly.

"No, Castigio. I'm going to the Kingdom of the Bright Morning Star with you! They'll all be quite safe now that Abaddon is locked up. I told them where the Shepherd went. They will meet us there at the Kingdom. I told them how to get there according to the instructions the Shepherd gave you."

"You are a true friend!" said Castigio. "I am honored to have you along."

Soot blushed.

Castigio noticed then how low the sun had slipped in the sky. "Soot, there is no time to lose. We must find Prince Zip while there is still daylight. We don't know when they might ship him away. Together they headed toward the docks to look for their friend.

The circus tent was just as Fetch-it had described it. Its appearance was deceiving. If one had not known it belonged to the pirates, one would have thought it was a wonderful fair set up for the town. Parked in a circle inside the big top was the caravan of decorated carts. Each cart had a gilded cage. Behind the bars of the cages hung velvet drapes, looking like the zoo of a rich king.

"Which cage is he in?" asked Soot as she peeped through a flap of the tent.

"I can't tell," said Castigio. "All the drapes are shut. We'll have to look in each one." So they did.

When they pulled the drapes on the first cage, they found it belonged to a grizzly brown bear. He growled at them and smacked at Castigio's helmet through the bars. Castigio promptly shut the drapes and hurried quietly to the next cage.

"I knew you were brave when I met you," Soot said. "But it seems you've gotten braver!"

Castigio did not know exactly why but he felt braver, so he said, "It seems you are right!" Then he walked up to the next cage with more boldness and threw back the drapes.

There, admiring himself in a hand mirror was Prince Zip! He was brushing out his yellow mane and was wearing his purple robe. He was so busy with his own vanity that he did not even notice them.

"Look at him! Will you?" whispered Soot. "That's disgusting!"

"Prince Zip! What are you doing in there?" exclaimed Castigio.

"Oh!" replied the startled lion cub. "What do you peasants want?"

"Peasants?" exclaimed Soot indignantly.

"We came to rescue you!" said Castigio before Soot could say any more.

"I don't want to be rescued. I'm the King of the Beasts and the star of the show! Now go away and leave me be!" said Prince Zip puffing out his little round chest.

"You're not any such thing!" contradicted the lamb.

"How would you know?" said Prince Zip.

260

## An Adventure

"Because it's plain to see that you're just a cat in a cage, and I'm as free as can be. You've been tricked and deceived! You couldn't roam free if you wanted to!" said Soot.

"Nonsense! I'm not going to listen to either of you. You've lied to me all along. Because of you peasants, my royal reputation was almost ruined!"

Castigio looked hurt. Soot was. She stuck her nose through the bars and bit his tail to show it! "There, if you didn't like that, catch me if you can!" she teased.

The lion cub raced to that side of the cage and lunged after her. "Lions kill lambs you know!" he roared in his most grown-up sounding voice.

"Since when?" asked Castigio in astonishment at Prince Zip's behavior. Instead of answering him, the cub took a flying leap at the lamb and smacked his head right into the bars of the cage. He stood up and weaved in a dizzy circle.

"You see, smarty cat!" said Soot. "You're not a king of anything! You're just a prisoner in a cage!"

Castigio reached a hand through the bars to steady him. "Abaddon just lied to you. This circus isn't real. It's just a vanity fair! It's a fake to keep you happy until they are through with you!"

"But that's not true! We parade through the streets and all the people pay us respect!" Prince Zip protested.

"They don't love you. They are just afraid of you, because the pirates might make you eat them!"

"Eat them?" said the lion cub distastefully.

"Yes! They'll starve you first and then turn you loose on them. You'll have no choice!" warned Castigio. "Then they'll ship you off to a zoo someplace on the other side of the world! You'll never ever see this island again."

"Ship me off?" asked the cub in disbelief.

"Yes! And we'll never ever see you again!" added the lamb for effect.

"Never?" asked the cub mournfully.

"Never!" Castigio assured him.

Prince Zip began to believe them and felt regretful for his prideful ways. "Please get me out of here. I don't want to kill lambs or anything! I just want to be free! If you'll take me with you to the Kingdom of the Morning Star, I'll go in any way they'll let me, whether they notice me or not. Please take me with you, I'll be good! I promise! Oh, please get me out of here. I don't want to be shipped away!" he begged.

"All right! We'll let you out if you promise not to play any more tricks or cause any more trouble!" said Castigio seeing his opportunity to correct the cub's bad behavior as well as to rescue him.

"I promise!" said Prince Zip.

Castigio began to look around for the latch on the cage and was about to open it when they heard a great commotion outside the tent. It was El Capitan and his band of men. They had caught the butchers and were coming to get the wild beasts for the banishing.

"Oh, hurry! Someone's coming!" cried the lion cub.

# An Adventure

"Stop thieves!" shouted the pirate as Castigio fiddled with the latch. "Someone is stealing my beasts!"

The earth seemed to shake as the pirate came rushing toward them. At the end of a leash by his side was the wolf. When Abaddon recognized them, he began to pull at his collar as if he would surely snap it in two.

Castigio didn't have time to think or run. Before he knew what was happening, the pirate was towering over him, waving his spear in the air. "So Castigio, my old fool! We meet again!" he laughed in an evil way and swung his weapon at Castigio's head. Castigio ducked under the wheel of the cage just in time. El Capitan's spear wedged in one of the spokes. He cursed and fumed and pulled at it.

Castigio knew it was useless to run so he shut his eyes tight and feared the worse. In that brief moment he could hear his heart beating. This reminded him to consult it as he had done when the pirate trapped him in the tavern the last time they met. "Use the sword!" was what his heart said.

"Of course! Bless the Morning Star! The sword!" he exclaimed and pulled it out of his bloomers.

No sooner had he done that than the pirate freed his spear. El Capitan and Castigio came face to face with weapons raised. All of a sudden, Castigio felt strangely courageous. The pirate was surprised. El Capitan tried to swing his spear again, but was met with a lightning quick stroke from Castigio's sword. Metal clashed against metal, and the pirate backed off a step. Again he tried. Again Castigio's sword blocked the blow! In shock El Capitan shrieked, "Curses! What magic have ye got there?"

"No magic!" said Castigio bravely. "Just power!"

"Castigio! What have ye done to yeself?" gasped the puzzled pirate.

"Nothing!" bragged the little Spaniard, "The Morning Star has done it all!"

"The Morning Star? I told ye never to mention that name to me again!" stuttered the pirate, for he was just as dumbfounded by the mention of it as he had been in the tavern when Castigio had sung him the strange account of its sighting.

Castigio marveled at the effect mentioning the Morning Star's name had on the pirate. "The Morning Star?" he asked. "Why, it won't hurt you."

"Don't say that!" El Capitan shrieked. "It's just a fairy tale ye and these villagers invented!"

"No, it is not! It's real. I've seen it!" Castigio proclaimed.

"It is not! I'll prove it!" yelled the pirate, and he lunged at Castigio again.

"Not by the powers of the Morning Star! No you won't!" Castigio shouted at him and blocked another blow with the sword.

"Stop saying that name!" shrieked the angry pirate.

"Morning Star!" said Castigio

"No!" screamed the pirate.

"Morning Star! Morning Star! Morning Star!" teased Castigio, amazed at the power it seemed to have over the evil villain. He wondered if he could hold him off forever like that. But he did not have the chance to find out. At that moment another crowd of people burst into the tent screaming, "There they are! Catch them! They let all the sheep go free!"

Castigio and Soot were trapped between the two mobs. Castigio was so shocked by their sudden entrance he forgot to keep up the sword. He had to duck again as the pirate swung at him.

"Castigio, what do we do now?" cried the lion and the lamb.

Above their heads a voice answered them. "Run!"

It was Fetch-it! He had sneaked into the tent unseen while the pirate was busy dueling with Castigio. With him were other orphans and beggars. He had rounded them up to help Castigio and Prince Zip escape after he had gotten away from the dream-snatchers. "It's going to be an adventure after all!" he shouted gleefully. And with that he opened the top of the cage for Prince Zip to spring out! Castigio, Soot and Prince Zip ran for the open flaps of the tent.

"I'll meet you in the Kingdom, brave knight!" the boy called after Castigio.

Castigio turned to wave just in time to see Fetch-it and his friends on top of the cages, busy unlatching them all! Animals were leaping out everywhere. Pirates and hirelings were screaming and running in every direction as the wild beasts pursued them.

Castigio and Soot were
trapped between the two mobs.

## An Adventure

Castigio felt proud as the three of them ran out of the tent and up the main street toward Tall Mountain. He was sure that Dreams would be proud of him. They had changed the village in one day. He was certain it would never be the same again. All that remained was to reach the Kingdom gates.

## 17

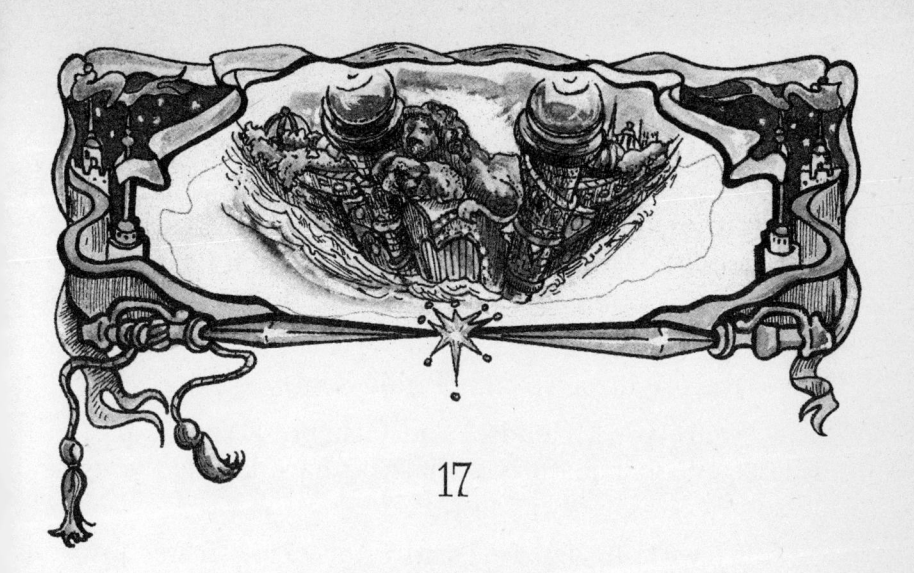

## At the Gates

Night had completely fallen by the time Castigio and his friends reached the first summit of Tall Mountain. The air was crisp and still. The sky over their heads was full of stars. It was peaceful to be up so high, away from the noise and fury of the village. Castigio was glad to be in the mountains again.

"Do you think it's safe to rest awhile?" Soot asked.

"I don't think the pirates will come all the way up here tonight!" said Prince Zip.

"It will take them awhile to recover from all that fuss at the tent! I hope they never do!" said Castigio. So they rested.

Prince Zip's eyes began filling with tears. "Castigio and Soot, I must beg your pardon and thank you from the bottom of my heart for rescuing me. It was so courageous!" He looked very grateful. Then he added, "How could I have been so blind? I didn't deserve for you to risk your lives to rescue me."

"You are most welcome!" said Soot.

"We're your friends!" said Castigio. "What is past is past. All that matters is that you have learned your lesson."

"I have! Oh, I have!" said Prince Zip. "It was just like Blue Cheetah said, my pride got the best of me! We all have a place in the Kingdom ahead of us. I can see that now. I am a guard. Soot is the Shepherd's friend. Castigio, you are a knight! Without each other we could never have made it this far!" exclaimed the lion cub who was now much wiser for the trial.

"I think he really means it!" said Soot, who was truly touched, for she had not cared about him much till then.

"Thank you, Soot," said Prince Zip sincerely. And to the Spaniard, "Castigio, you are a real friend, true blue!"

"It was an honor, Your Majesty," Castigio blushed.

"But we must be on our way again!" said Castigio, standing up. Actually all the sentimental compliments embarrassed him, because he did not feel worthy.

Soot and Prince Zip followed him.

"Castigio, you were even braver than usual! I hardly thought you were yourself!" exclaimed Soot as they walked along.

"Yes!" agreed Prince Zip. "You fought that pirate like a true knight!"

"I did?" asked the Spaniard cautiously.

"Yes! Weren't you scared?" asked Soot.

"No, I wasn't really," mused Castigio. "Me – the greatest coward I know! Imagine that!"

"Coward? You're no coward, Castigio! Why, that mean old pirate meant to kill you! Weren't you afraid to die?" asked Soot.

"Why no, Soot. I should have been, but I wasn't. Was I?" asked Castigio. "It must have been the power of the Morning Star! The pirate was more afraid of the Star than I was of him!"

"He sure was!" said Prince Zip.

"Well, I was afraid of him!" said Soot.

"What scared you most?" asked Prince Zip curiously.

"I thought he would kill us all!" she said trembling.

"Are you afraid to die?" asked Castigio, "Don't you remember what Dreams told us?"

"Who?" asked the lion cub.

"Someone we met, after you ran away from us," explained Castigio. "She told us that only those who believe in the power of the Star can enter through its gates."

"What's its power?" asked Prince Zip.

"She said the Morning Star can make all things brand new, even dead things!" said Soot.

"Then why don't you believe it?"

"I would if I could have seen that Star like you did, Castigio, or maybe if I'd seen that dead man get up like in your vision. But I can't even imagine it," Soot said. "I can't even think of what the secret city and the Kingdom must be like."

Castigio felt sorry for her and tried to think of something to say. "Well, you have seen the Shepherd and you know the Kingdom is where he lives. Right?"

"Yes, of course!" said the lamb.

"Then that means you believe there is such a place!" said Castigio helpfully.

"Yes!" said Soot.

"And you've seen the power of the sword of the Morning Star?"

"Yes, I have!" said the lamb excitedly.

"Then you must use your faith to understand the rest that you have not seen!" offered Castigio kindly. She seemed to be satisfied with that.

"I believe in all of it!" said Prince Zip. "I have my wonderful cape to prove it! There must be such a place and such a Star with such a power!" He spun around to show off the grand purple cape that he was still wearing around his neck.

As he did, Prince Zip suddenly let out a howling cry, for a great gray buzzard had spotted his cape from the sky. The robe had tickled its fancy, and it was soaring down with all its might to snatch it!

"The gray buzzards!" yelled Castigio. "Prince Zip, watch out for his talons! They've got poison in them!" he warned, recalling what the Shepherd had said.

## At the Gates

Prince Zip could not hear him. He was flapping about frantically under the cape, as the buzzard swooped down to carry it off. The buzzard had not realized the cape was attached to somebody, but tried to carry off the lion cub as well. Castigio rushed to help him, pulling out his sword. With one slash he cut the cape free from Prince Zip's neck. The buzzard seemed satisfied to carry the cape off alone.

"Oh, my inheritance! It's gone!" Prince Zip moaned.

"Don't be silly!" said the lamb. "How do you really even know it was yours?"

"I don't know, but the owls that found me in the forest said I had one just like that. I felt somehow that I had found it. It made me feel like I had a part of the Kingdom," explained the sad little cub.

"Your inheritance will surely be much greater than one robe, Your Royal Highness. Cheer up!" said Castigio, "If we are near the buzzard's nest, then we must be very, very close to the Kingdom now!"

Prince Zip stopped pouting and looked up at the mountain. The three could see a narrow ridge above their heads and some cliffs off to the right. Just then another figure of a bird soared across the sky. They all ducked.

"Don't worry!" sighed Castigio. "It's a white eagle! They won't hurt you, only the buzzards. Come on! We are very close now!" Soot and Prince Zip were greatly relieved.

Huffing and puffing, the trio of friends climbed the steep peak and came at last to the top. The sight on the other side was breathtaking to behold! Shining in its fullest glory was the brilliant Morning Star! This time they all could see it.

Stretched out beyond them was a pasture that sloped steeply down to a jagged cliff. On the other side was the churning, rushing river and behind it the pink walls of the marvelous fortress which contained the city and reached farther than the eye could see. Jewels sparkled in the towers of the city as the light of the Star arched in many rainbows across the width of the river and the Kingdom's gates.

Inside the fortress lay the city, carved out of pure sapphires and trimmed with gold and every precious metal. Pennants of silk, hanging from the windows of many mansions, waved in a gentle breeze. In the center a splashing fountain sprang up higher than the city's tallest buildings and the mountain's highest peaks!

The sight was far richer than anyone could have imagined. It would have taken ages to study and note every detail. The towers alone were carved from top to bottom with the same stories that appeared on the sheathe of the sword but with a great deal more intricacy!

From throughout the wonderful place came the sound of the most magnificent music! It seemed to pour out of every window, each rock in the walls, and from the river and the fountain too! Castigio was certain at last that it was the same song Dreams had piped on her flute each day. He knew too it was the music the streams and his own heart had been singing everywhere on the island, only this time it was a thousand times louder! Yet mysteriously enough, they had not heard it until they crossed over the mountain.

## At the Gates

Down in the city were a strange people as beautiful as Dreams had been. The entire vision beckoned them each to enter.

"Oh, Castigio! I believe it all!" whispered Soot reverently. Castigio smiled, but he could not speak a word for he was awestruck.

"What are we waiting for?" quipped Prince Zip. "Our inheritance is calling us! Let's go!" He was about to bound off down the slope when a gravelly voice spoke behind them.

"What's the rush?"

They all spun around in time to see Abaddon's head pop up from a hole hidden in the cliff behind the ridge where they stood. Somehow he had escaped El Capitan in the confusion and had speedily found his way through the network of tunnels to cut them off at the gates.

"Abaddon!" shrieked the lamb.

"You can't stop us!" shouted Castigio. "Get back, or I'll be forced to kill you with my sword!" He waved it fiercely at the wolf! Abaddon snarled and slid back down into the cave until only his red eyes could be seen, glowing in the darkness.

"You showed him!" cheered Prince Zip. "Let's go!"

"Not so fast!" snarled the wolf. "I have something that you might not want to leave behind!" and he hissed a hideous laugh.

"You're a liar!" yelled Castigio boldly. "There's nothing we could want from that side of the mountain anymore! Whatever it is, you can keep it! We won't need it!"

"Have it your way," said the wolf in a sly voice.

"Wait, Castigio!" begged Soot. "He gave up too easily. He's up to something. Find out what he wants! Please!"

Castigio did not want to be bothered. The lure of the Morning Star was so strong he could hardly stand it. Just then there was a dreadful bleating behind them, and Soot turned to see what it was.

"Castigio! My flock! He's captured my whole flock!" cried the lamb. "We can't let him have them. I just can't go in without them!"

Castigio and Prince Zip saw the flock coming over the ridge. The whimpering lambs were held captive by a vicious pack of wolves, each nearly as large as Abaddon their leader.

"We can't let them have them! They'll eat them alive!" sobbed the lamb.

As much as Castigio wanted to go into the Kingdom, he found he could not. Soot had been his faithful friend through the whole journey. He had given her his pledge to be faithful too. She had believed in him when no one else had ever tried. He could not let her down now. Besides, he dreaded the thought of slaughtered sheep!

"What will it take to set them free?" Castigio yelled at the wolf.

"Come over here and fight me for them! Just you and I. Winner takes all!" bargained the wolf.

"Why don't you come out here, where I can see you then?" challenged Castigio.

## At the Gates

"I don't have to. The prize is on my side," sneered the wolf. In truth, he was very fearful of the Morning Star and didn't want to come any closer. But Castigio didn't know it.

"Be careful, Castigio! I think it's a trick!" warned Prince Zip.

"Where do we fight?" shouted Castigio. He was so angry, that for the first time in his life he had forgotten to be scared.

"Send the other two away first. Make them cross the river. When I know they are on the other side and won't cross back to help you, we'll fight!" said the wolf.

Castigio, Soot and Prince Zip huddled together for a conference. "Castigio, the river is too dangerous to cross by ourselves," said Soot.

"I think I could get a running start and leap across it to the towers," said Prince Zip. "But Soot is not bouncy like I am. We would need your help. He knows it too, the sly devil! It's another trick to drown us."

"Oh, Castigio, I could never cross that river anyway," sobbed the lamb with fright as she stared at it. "I never noticed it at first, but now that he's mentioned it, I don't see how I could have ever hoped to cross it in the first place. There's no way for me to enter the Kingdom after all! I've come all this way for nothing! Just go on and save yourselves. It's me he really wants. Lamb is his favorite dish!" sobbed Soot.

"Nothing doing!" exclaimed the lion cub loyally.

"We won't do it!" said Castigio firmly. "There just has to be a way into the Kingdom for you. We'll search

277

until we find it. Blue Cheetah said you would get to the arms of your Shepherd, and you will!"

Soot's eyes became wide.

"Castigio! Watch out!" she cried.

While the three had been conferring, Abaddon and his pack of wolves had been creeping as close to the edge of the ridge as they dared, and from overhead a terrifying flock of buzzards had joined them to divide the spoils.

"Run for your lives! To the river! You'll be safer on the banks!" Castigio yelled as he drew his sword to face Abaddon and the pack.

Standing before them, he froze, not knowing where to strike first. Swooping down were the buzzards with their outstretched talons of poison, and circling in to him was the vicious snarling wolf pack!

Castigio's heart was pounding so loud he couldn't think. Then he heard a familiar chorus sounding deep inside. He felt it rise up through his soul and burst into a triumphant song at the top of his lungs.

> **We have drunk from living waters clear,**
> **Mortal wounds, we keep no more!**
> **Oh, Morning Star, whose beams are dear,**
> **You have changed the battle score!**

It was the victory song he had heard the band of men singing in the fountain the first time he saw the Kingdom.

Suddenly his magnificent sword began to glow with a white light, and the earth near the cave and the ridge began to tremble. He started to fight as he sang! The shaking knocked Abaddon off the ridge and he

Suddenly his magnificent sword began to glow.

rolled head over heels all the way down to the bank of the river, far below where Prince Zip stood cheering Castigio on.

Castigio took off down the hill to finish him off waving the sword above his head. As he ran he suddenly heard a curious yelping behind him and looked back. The wolf pack was madly retreating! A shower of pebbles pursued them, then the shout of children's voices. Popping over the ridge was a familiar face. Fetch-it had made it to the end of the adventure after all. With his slingshot and his friends, they were driving the wolf pack off!

"Go get him, Castigio! We'll finish off the buzzards for you!" Fetch-it yelled.

Castigio waved the sword and charged down the rest of the hill. Abaddon was staggering to his feet when he saw Castigio coming. He was shocked to see the terrifying sight that met his eyes because Castigio no longer was the cowering fool Abaddon first encountered, but was every inch the mighty warrior. His face was set with determination, his armor glowed in the light of the Morning Star. Lightnings flashed about the weapon Castigio raised high above his head.

"No, not that sword!" Abaddon howled as he recognized it being that which had pierced him years before by the hand of the Pilgrim. He recalled its unmatched power and snarled as he circled around the cliff and looked for a way out.

Below him was the raging river, above him the blinding brilliance of the Star, and before him Castigio and the sword and an army of orphans screaming in his ears. There was no way out.

## At the Gates

Flashing his red eyes wildly in search of an escape, Abaddon snarled a warning for Castigio to retreat, then arched his back and prepared to lunge. The wolf leaped. Just as Castigio and Abaddon came face to face, Castigio thrust forth the sword and plunged it deep into the heart of the great black beast. Jerking back the weapon, Castigio stood aside and watched in astonishment.

With a mortal wound and one last howl, Abaddon fell over the cliff, the roaring river washing him downstream. He was never to be seen again!

"Hooray! Bless the Morning Star! Castigio – our hero!" shouted the orphans as they rushed down the hill to meet him, followed by the lambs, who bleated out a grand cheer! There was great rejoicing! "Abaddon is dead! He's dead!" they all shouted. "And we're at the gates of the Kingdom at last!'

"How did you ever find us?" asked Castigio, when Fetch-it caught up to him.

"After you left, we freed all the animals. Then we waited to see what would happen. The pirates and the hirelings and the beasts began fighting each other! It was marvelous! But then we noticed that the black wolf had broken his collar in all the battling and was getting away. We knew he would be after you. So we took our chance to run away and climbed the mountain. That's when we saw the wolf pack encircling those lambs and decided to corner them with our slingshots! Just when we caught up to them, we found you and this wonderful place! It really isn't just a fairy tale!" explained Fetch-it. "I believe everything I ever dreamed about it!"

"So do I," said Castigio putting his arm around the boy's shoulders. "What are we waiting for friends? Let's cross the river and get into our Kingdom!"

"Oh! No! Castigio! Look!" cried Prince Zip in a very solemn voice. Slowly, he pointed toward a still small figure lying in the grass.

"What is it, Your Royal Highness?" asked Castigio, slapping him on the back, still in a joyful gesture.

"It's...It's...It's...." The lion cub could not finish. Then Castigio saw where he pointed.

"Soot!" wailed the Spaniard dropping to his knees. "Soot! Soot! Oh, Soot! My dear little Lambkin!" he sobbed. She was dead!

Castigio reached down and picked up her lifeless body in his arms. He hugged her and cried. He could not believe she had left them – and on the very shores of the Kingdom.

"How could this be?" he said, holding her up to the Morning Star as it still shone on them so peacefully and still. There was no answer.

Castigio set her back down on the hillside, where the pasture grew up the slope. As he did, the rest of the lambs, the orphans and Prince Zip gathered around in mourning. How could it have happened? Castigio noticed a mark on her thigh. Then he realized that while they were fighting the wolves, she had bravely battled a buzzard. Its deadly talons had clawed her and taken away her life.

"We've failed her," Castigio sobbed. "I promised to take her to her Shepherd, and she never made it." They all grieved.

## At the Gates

"You brought her as far as anyone could," a strong but kind voice said.

Castigio looked up into the gentle eyes of her loving Shepherd. He had come for her at last.

"Oh, forgive me, sir!" he wept. "I could have asked you to help me find her the night we met. But I was too embarrassed to say I'd lost her then and failed her there as well. So I lied. If I hadn't then none of this would have happened, and she'd be alive in your arms. She'd be happy right now!"

"And if I hadn't run off to the circus and left her...," Prince Zip cried, "then so much time wouldn't have been wasted and we would have gotten here sooner and...." He couldn't go on. He felt truly responsible and sorry.

"My friends, it is not your fault," said the kind Shepherd. "Soot was willing to let you all go through the gates without her because she feared the very last steps of the journey. For her there was no other way." He knelt down and picked her up.

"What way is there now?" sobbed Castigio and Prince Zip together. "Soot's dead, and we should bury her here in this pasture where she looked over the city."

"No need for that," said the Shepherd calmly. He picked up the lamb and began to walk toward the bank of the river.

"Where are you taking her?" cried Castigio demanding to know!

"Why didn't you come here sooner and rescue her when she was alive?" sobbed Prince Zip.

283

"I am taking her home. You will see her when you get there," said the Shepherd.

"What is he talking about?" asked Prince Zip.

The Shepherd turned to Castigio, "Have you forgotten the power of the Morning Star?" he said. He left them wondering a moment, then carried Soot to the bank and into the river. As he did, a magnificent beam of the Bright Morning Star shot out to greet him – as if some secret signal had operated it – and the raging river parted to either side of the gate.

Castigio and Prince Zip stood staring in amazement. The others gave a shout of joy and, being the eager children they were, ran right behind the Shepherd through the gates.

Prince Zip watched them, not knowing what he should do. He was mixed up with grief and wonder and joy, all at the same time. But as the last child passed through the gate, he noticed a carving above it. There, in the stone, was a statue of the lion and the lamb! They were lying down together on a royal throne and seemed to be guarding the gate!

"My destiny! My throne! My inheritance! Castigio, look!" shouted Prince Zip. "Don't you see? Soot and I have a throne together in the Kingdom! It's been foretold in stone just as the carvings on the sword foretold our journey! The Morning Star makes all things new! You said it! Even dead things! In there she will live again! Soot will be alive! She'll be waiting for us to join her!"

Castigio's sad face began to brighten. He realized this must be true! He remembered the dead man brought back to life in the fountain.

## At the Gates

Prince Zip could wait for him no longer. "I'll meet you on the other side!" he cried and bounded over the bank and disappeared through the gates.

Castigio watched as a royal guard of lions and lionesses came out to welcome Prince Zip with his very own purple robe!

Castigio could not explain his own hesitation. He stood a moment more gazing at the Kingdom before him. Then he began to walk reverently toward the bank of the river. Just as he set his foot down on the ground where the river had parted, someone called his name.

"Castigio! Wait! There is something more you must know before you go in!"

He turned to see that the voice was that of the tottering Pilgrim. He was tripping over his beard as usual and walking crookedly as he came over the ridge toward Castigio. Around his neck was a blooming garland of roses from his gardens and under his arm was Castigio's coveted helmet!

"Are you surprised to see me, Turtle?" the Pilgrim wheezed with a twinkle in his eye.

"Yes! I thought the wolf had eaten you!" Castigio answered.

"He almost did. But we overturned the soup upon us in our rumble. He got the worst of it and went screaming up the chimney. That's the last I saw of him. After that my garden grew so well and I felt so happy, I decided to seek out the Kingdom of the Bright Morning Star once more. I found it and you just in time!"

285

"Just in time?" asked Castigio.

"Yes, my friend. You have an important decision to make!"

"I do?"

"Are you ready to pass through the gates of the Kingdom?" asked the Pilgrim balancing on one foot.

"Yes! Of course! I've come so far and gone through so much to get here!" answered Castigio.

"Did you know that once you cross over you cannot come back?"

"No! But what does it matter?" asked Castigio.

"For me it is not so important, for I am very old for this side anyway. But you do have time left," said the Pilgrim.

"Time for what?" asked Castigio.

"Time to do the work that Dreams commissioned you to do."

"How do you know what she said to me?" Castigio asked in surprise.

"On my way out of the gardens I saw and spoke with her on the same hill you did," the Pilgrim said. "This time I took the path I did not choose so long ago. Dreams told me she had asked you to awaken the sleeping hearts of the people in the villages and tell them your dreams."

"I did that, and the boy I told is on the other side of that gate right now waiting for me!" answered Castigio impatiently.

"Only one boy?" asked the ancient man. "Only one?"

"He brought a few friends!" said Castigio defensively.

"Only a few? What about the other villagers?" poked the Pilgrim.

"Um..." is all Castigio could say. He felt uncomfortable. He looked again at the gates of the Kingdom. He thought of seeing Soot alive and Prince Zip with her reigning together over the gates. He thought of Fetch-it and the Fountain of Youth inside. How long it seemed that he had already waited to get there at last. How could he be denied?

As Castigio stared out over the city, the waters in the river began slowly to cover the path where they had parted. He realized that any minute the gates would close again.

"What will I get if I go back to tell them? Will I have another chance at this?" he begged to know, for by now the Pilgrim had done his job, and the decision was weighing heavily on Castigio's heart.

"Yes! Next time it will be easier, and when it is right for you to join us, you will know. If you stay, you will be a full-fledged knight of the Kingdom of the Bright Morning Star. You will be like Blue Cheetah and know things sometimes. You will win great battles, and discover more enemies left to conquer besides Abaddon. When you are all through, there will be a great reward waiting inside for you! It is well worth the price!"

"And what will happen if I go with you now?"

"We will welcome you with joy, and you will be with your friends. But you will never know the others you left behind."

"Will they get into the Kingdom later? Will the Morning Star help them as he did me?" Castigio asked, hoping for the sort of answer that would ease his conscience.

"Maybe a few, but mostly, no," replied the Pilgrim.

Castigio looked at the river. It was closing faster now. He was sweating harder under the pressure. "What to do?"

The Pilgrim waited. Then Castigio heard the voice of his heart saying, "Stay." Oh, it was such a final little voice, but always right as it had proven thus far.

"It's up to you, Turtle!" said the Pilgrim. "Here is your helmet. I thought you should have it since I stole it from you. I'm sorry."

"No. You keep it," Castigio told him. "It's a habit I already gave up." The Pilgrim shook his head and was not sure he understood.

"Are you coming? I must go," said the Pilgrim.

Castigio shook his head, then followed the Pilgrim back to the river's edge. There he stood watching as the Pilgrim waved goodby and teeter-tottered through the gates as the river came crashing together again. Castigio felt a little pain of disappointment as he went back up the hill. He was certain that he had done the right thing, but his heart was heavy because he knew not what lay ahead nor how he would face the days without his friends. On the ridge Castigio turned back for one more look at the Kingdom.

Off in the distance he saw the city's magnificent towers and silky banners twirling in the air above the golden streets and wonderful fountain! Oh! The fountain! There in its basin the Shepherd lay Soot. Though far off, Castigio recognized her. He watched in amazement as a beam of the Morning Star swept across the sky and touched her lifeless form. First there was a stirring and then a splash! Soot came to life and began prancing about in the center of them as good as new!

Castigio's heart leaped for joy as he saw the waters begin to swirl and bubble around her. The children who had gone on before him went playing and leaping to her side, splashing with merry delight!

A great flood of peace swept over Castigio. A bright ray of the Morning Star shot past him also as if to show approval. Castigio lifted his sword to the sky in a salute and was surprised to feel that his sleeve was too tight and his bloomers too small! "What on earth?" He looked down at his stockings and saw not a wrinkle. His helmet did not roll off his nose as he looked down. It stayed on his head where it belonged. He reached up a hand to feel what held it in place and found that he was no longer bald!

"Mercy sakes! What has happened to me?" he asked himself. He put his hands in front of his face and saw that they were smooth and youthful! Then he knew the answer.

"The Morning Star makes all things new!" Castigio exclaimed. "By Glory! He's given me a second chance at life!"

He glanced back once more at the Kingdom to look at his friends, but could not see them anywhere. Only the children played in the fountain. What had become of the lion and the lamb?

Searching for the Morning Star

For a moment Castigio fretted as he searched for a sign of them. Then to his complete delight he spied Prince Zip pulling himself up over the Kingdom gates. Planting a clumsy paw firmly on the top, he heaved his little round belly up as well and reached back down for his tail. Castigio rejoiced to see Soot clinging to it, being pulled up after. There they stood, the best of friends at last, waving to him together as if to say, "Go tell the others and we shall see you soon!"

Right up there on the mountain he danced a jig for joy! All his dreams had come true and his heart nearly burst with a new song that he could hardly wait to share. With a heart full of courage, faith and joy, Castigio lifted his sword once more and turned toward the village below.

Saluting the Morning Star, he felt every inch a noble knight!

Saluting the Morning Star, Castigio

felt every inch a noble Knight.

If you would like to become
a knight of the Morning Star, write:

Sheldon's Limited Editions

c/o Harrison House Publishers

P. O. Box 35035

Tulsa, OK 74153

Shelli Jones – author, illustrator, songwriter and minister has traveled in Europe and throughout the United States singing and teaching. As a missionary, she has traveled to Guatemala to work in children's crusades. There she developed a pantomime troupe, designing and helping construct the puppets. Also as a missionary, Shelli has traveled to Israel, Russia and Finland ministering to adults as well as children.

A graduate of Rhode Island School of Design with a BFA in Illustration and Film Animation, Shelli has worked as a freelance illustrator and animation artist for television commercials.